Mountain bikes: maintenance and repair

Mountain bikes maintenance and repair

John Stevenson

SBL Springfield Books Limited

© 1991 John Stevenson

Published by Springfield Books Limited,
Norman Road, Denby Dale, Huddersfield
HD8 8TH West Yorkshire, England

First edition 1991

British Library Cataloguing in Publication Data
Stevenson, John
    Mountain bikes: maintenance and repair
    I. Title
    629.28772

ISBN 1 85688 018 4

Acknowledgements

The author and publishers would like to thank
Brant Richards and Steve Snowling for their help
with the text.

Photography

The cover picture is by Nigel Jackson (Stockfile)
and the back cover picture by Steve Behr (Stockfile)
The pictures on pages 2, 84, 85, 86, 87, 88, 89,
90, 91, 100, 109, 110, 121, 130, 132, 138, 142,
143 and 144 are by Steve Behr (Stockfile)
The pictures on pages 99, 113, 114, 118 and 119 are
by Stewart Clarke (ActionPact)
The pictures on pages 8 and 82 are by Neil Munns
The picture on page 137 is by Brant Richards
All other photography is by Graham Watson

Design: Chris Hand Design for Print
Illustrations: Mark Greaves
Typesetting: Armitage Typo/Graphics, Huddersfield
Printed and bound in England by
Butler & Tanner Limited

Contents

1: Introduction

The mountain bike has been one of the phenomena of recent years. Its durability, practicality and comfort have brought millions of people to cycling who would never have considered riding a bike, on or off road, and the resulting boom in world bike sales has funded a significant improvement in the quality and performance of the equipment that is available to all types of cyclist.

Whether you race, commute, tour or just ride a mountain bike for the sheer joy of getting out into the countryside, this manual is intended to help you get more out of your mountain bike by keeping it in the best possible mechanical condition.

At its heart, the mountain bike is still a machine and like any machine it needs a certain amount of regular attention to keep it working at its best. Regularly maintaining your mountain bike has lots of benefits, besides just keeping it working properly.

First of all, of course, there's the financial factor. A good mechanic charges a good hourly rate, and although good mechanics are fast (that's one of the things that makes them good mechanics) it's still cheaper to maintain your own bike, provided you can spare the evening that any routine jobs will take.

The other half of the financial equation is that a well-maintained bike costs less to run in the long term. Worn bike parts cause secondary wear to other components if you don't replace them promptly. A classic example of this is the chain, which will wear the sprockets and chainrings out to the point where a new chain will not work with them. If the chain is replaced before it is too worn, the sprockets and rings last much longer.

Secondly, there's the certainty of knowing that your bike is working right because *you* checked it over last. During my brief and unstartling racing career I turned up for an event with a bike which had just had a new rear wheel built by a colleague who was an ace wheel-builder, and he'd put the tyre back on for me and pumped it up harder than I was used to. I forgot to check the tyre pressure before I got to the start line and spent the first lap of the race getting bounced around by the over-hard tyre until I finally stopped to let out a few psi. If I'd inflated it myself I'd have had no such problem.

1988 World champion Mike Kloser takes this attitude to its logical extreme, and can frequently be seen stripping and reassembling his bike in the hotel the evening before a race until he is completely happy that it is working perfectly. Lining up at the start and being absolutely certain that your bike works perfectly leaves your mind clear to concentrate on racing. As Mike puts it, 'You don't want to be there on the start line wondering whether your bike's gonna make it.'

Thirdly, knowing how your bike works and how to fix it is extremely useful if it breaks down while you're out on the trails. A minor mechanical problem can become a major disaster if you're miles from nowhere with no tools.

Riders who carry a basic tool kit and know how to use it will also find they get invited on more rides!

Lastly, working on your bike is intrinsically satisfying. Learning how to use the tools of the bike mechanic's trade is an enjoyable process and the end result, a fund of knowledge that allows you to bail your friends out of mechanical troubles that they consider insoluble, is extremely useful (and can be lucrative; most professional mechanics are self-taught). I recently had to service a badly jammed Shimano hub, the result of misadjustment by a so-called mechanic who didn't know what he was doing. When I started the part looked like a write-off, and the owner was contemplating buying a new hub and having the wheel rebuilt. Stripping the thing down proved difficult, but once we'd got it apart the fault was actually quite simple and easy to cure. What I really enjoyed about this job was not the mere fact of helping out a friend, but the satisfaction of resurrecting an apparently terminal component.

Despite these advantages most people seem afraid to tackle even the most basic jobs on their bikes. I've seen bikes checked into dealer's workshops for the most minor problems; maladjusted gears, misaligned stems, punctures. There is a myth that bike mechanics have some sort of mystical 'mechanical aptitude' which gives them a supernatural rapport with the cold steel and aluminium of modern mountain bikes. While a few such individuals undoubtedly exist (they are called wheel-builders, and we will look at their skills in a later chapter) anyone can pick up the necessary mechanical skills to do most of the routine jobs on a mountain bike, given the right tools and a little time and practice. I was utterly ham-fisted in 'technical' subjects at school and I still run a mile when presented with a wood plane or a precision filing job but I can tweak bike components as well as anyone, though usually not as quickly as some.

I didn't actually start doing my own maintenance until I was in my late teens. The biking bug was beginning to bite deep and I was an impecunious student. I learnt from necessity because if I didn't do my own repairs I couldn't afford to ride. Within a couple of years I was working as a part-time mechanic in a bike shop.

Nevertheless, I'm not a 'natural' mechanic. I didn't dismantle my dad's car when I was twelve, then reassemble it so it worked perfectly and *then* make a profit on the two boxes of parts I had left over, or build model aeroplanes that covered ridiculous distances, and you don't need to have either. Anyone can learn how to fix bikes. Anyone. The vital things are tools and time.

We'll look at tool kits later, but the other half of that pairing is time. I know people who can quite cheerfully stand there with a brazing torch in hand putting the final touches to the frame that they are going touring on next day, but this is not a sensible attitude for a rookie mechanic to take. Give yourself plenty of time for any job, preferably an open-ended amount of it. Nothing is worse than attempting to adjust a hub fifteen minutes before you're going riding; every attempt at haste will just make you more clumsy. Do it the day before, preferably while there's a bike shop open so you can get help if you get irretrievably stuck.

Another myth about the ability to repair and maintain bikes is that it's a secondary sexual characteristic, that the only people who can possibly be good mechanics are men, because the ability to wield a spanner is somehow passed from generation to generation on the Y chromosome. This is clearly nonsense, and it's encouraging to see that the number of female pro mechanics has grown dramatically over the last few years.

I used to work at a bike shop where my partner and mechanic was Rachel Southgate. Like me, Rachel started learning mechanics while she was at college. 'I started fixing my own bike after watching other people fix it for me, and realising it really wasn't that difficult. Once you've seen things done, you realise that they're quite easy and then it's just a matter of having the right tools and the confidence to tackle things yourself.'

Rachel learned by watching other riders, and by hanging out at her local bike shop. You can learn a lot by being a bike shop hanger-on, and she had the good luck to be able to ask someone if she got into problems. This is a common way to learn – most mechanics are happy to tell you how to do things (as long as they're not too busy) – it gives them a chance to display the knowledge that they've accumulated over the years.

Rachel teaches a bike maintenance class for women and comments that the commonest problem she encounters among her pupils is simple ignorance about the innards of bike components. From the outside, a bottom bracket bearing can be a complete mystery, but as she says 'once you get it apart, and see that it's just a cup and a cone – there's nothing you can break , and you can just take your time and fiddle with it until it's right – then you get more confident.'

She adds a crucial point about maintenance: 'I've taught a lot of people how to recognise faults. I think most people would be able to do a job, but they don't realise they've got a problem until it's too late. You've got to learn that a particular rattle can mean that your headset is loose.'

This book will, I hope, help you learn what a particular rattle means, and how you should fix it.

2: Tools of the trade

It's a truism that the bad workman blames his or her tools, but the flipside of this cliché is that nobody can do a good job without reasonably good quality tools. This doesn't mean that the rookie mechanic should rush out and spend hundreds of pounds on a full set of Park or Campagnolo tools, just that if you are going to make an investment in a tool kit it's worth buying good quality.

Tools fall into two categories: 'normal' tools, which you can get from any good hardware shop and which includes spanners, Allen keys, screwdrivers and pliers; and 'specialist' tools, which are unique to bikes and can be had from well-stocked dealers.

The extent and quality of the tools you buy will depend on the level of repairs you want to attempt, and I group tool kits into five classes; basic, intermediate, advanced, professional and trail.

The basic tool kit

A basic tool kit contains what you need to adjust and maintain all parts of the bike except the bearings and wheels. With basic tools you will be able to adjust gears and brakes and replace the expendable parts of these systems – that is the cables, brake blocks and gear jockey wheels – and the components themselves. Basic tools also allow you to adjust or replace the handlebar and stem, the saddle and of course the tyres and inner tubes.

This is all many riders will need. Jobs like dismantling and regreasing the bearings of the hubs, headset and bottom bracket need doing infrequently and can be left to a bike shop. The basic tool kit is the minimum you need to work efficiently and effectively on your bike, and usually contains the following:

- Combination spanners: 8mm, 9mm, 10mm
- Socket spanners: 8mm, 9mm, 10mm
- Allen keys: 2mm, 2.5mm, 3mm, 4mm, 5mm, 6mm
- Combination pliers
- Cable cutters
- Small cross-head screwdriver
- Small flat-blade screwdriver
- Large flat-blade screwdriver
- 8in adjustable spanner
- Cable puller (optional)
- Chain cleaner
- Tyre levers
- Puncture repair kit
- WD40
- Lubricant
- Solvent
- Grease
- Barrier cream
- Hand cleaner
- Workstand
- Third hand tool

A typical basic tool kit containing tools, grease, lubricants, solvent and hand cleaner

Almost all of these can be obtained from a good tool shop.

Combination spanners have a ring spanner on one end and an open spanner on the other, and are the most versatile general purpose spanner. Socket spanners with extension bars and maybe even a universal joint are useful for getting into awkward places, and come in handy when you need to get two spanners the same size onto a cable clamp. Alternatively, many bike shops stock a Y-spanner which has 8mm, 9mm and 10mm sockets in one easily handled unit.

Other sizes of Allen keys than those listed here are sometimes encountered, though more often on accessories and ancillary components than on bikes themselves. These six will do for almost all jobs on the bike itself; if you come across a component that needs an Allen key you don't have, take it

down to your friendly local tool shop and make sure you get the right size.

Combination pliers have a cutting edge and square jaws, with a rounded grip section in the jaws.

Good cable cutters are a must. The cutting edge on pliers is not usually good enough for brake cable, and tends to crush it. A bike shop will be able to get you a set of SunTour's excellent cable cutters, which are reasonably priced and will stand up to years of use.

A six or eight inch adjustable spanner is always useful to have in case you encounter an unusual nut or bolt size. Don't skimp on this tool: good ones are a joy to use, cheap ones are nasty. Bahco make the best.

A cable puller, sometimes called a fourth hand tool, is not essential (you can use pliers) but it does make the job of adjusting the tension in brake and gear cables much easier.

A chain cleaner like those from Vetta and Park is the lazy mechanic's way of getting the dirt out of a chain; they're incredibly useful if you ride off-road a lot.

Tyre levers and a puncture repair kit can be obtained from bike shops, as can good quality water-resistant bicycle grease, like that made by Nimrod, Cyclon or Park, and a medium grade spray lubricant like Cyclon MTB, Superspray Lube MTB or LPS3. WD40 is very useful for driving out water from splashed parts and releasing seized threads, but should not be used on its own as a lubricant; it's too light.

Solvents are a thorny issue. They are used to remove dirt which is too ingrained to wash off easily, but most solvents are toxic, both to people and the environment, and eventually they get washed down the drain. For this reason I use Cyclon's biodegradable chain cleaner, which is also non-toxic. The distributors claim you can drink it; I haven't tried this, and I don't imagine it tastes very good.

Barrier cream is available from auto supply shops and good tool shops. It forms a protective layer which prevents oil from soaking into your skin and clogging up your pores, and makes it easier to wash off afterwards.

Good hand cleaner is essential; who wants to go around with dirt ingrained in their hands after a maintenance session? Swarfega is the most famous mechanic's hand cleaner, though Tufanega (from the same company) is very effective and less harsh on the skin. We used it in the bike shop where I learned bike repair because the head mechanic was allergic to Swarfega.

I've left the workstand until last because it is not essential – you can lean your bike against the wall or turn it upside-down – but it does allow you easy access to all parts of the bike, making basic jobs like replacing gear cables much easier. Having the bike held firmly is a real help when you get to the bearing-adjusting jobs which the intermediate tool kit allows you to tackle.

A couple of hooks on chains from the garage roof is a reasonable second-best if you can't afford a workstand; it holds the bike up at a sensible level so you can work on it.

The intermediate tool kit

The next level of tool kit allows you to get at the bearings in the headset, hubs and bottom bracket to grease, replace and service them. These tools are relatively expensive and are not needed very often, unless you ride a lot, in which case they are an investment that will quickly pay for itself. Raleigh team pro Paul Hinton reckons that he completely rebuilds the bearings on his bike every month when the weather is bad. During one very wet summer, Paul was stripping and rebuilding bearings on a weekly basis, because every race happened under appallingly wet conditions.

Being able to service the bearings will allow you to keep your bike in the best possible working order, and you will learn quickly when a component needs attention. Regular replacement of the grease in bearings will prolong their life, and save you money in the long run.

These tools are:

- **Headset spanners (two)**
- **Fixed cup spanner**
- **Lockring spanner**
- **Adjustable cup (peg) spanner**
- **15mm pedal spanner**
- **2 x 13/14mm cone spanners**
- **2 x 15/16mm cone spanner**
- **17/18mm cone spanner**
- **Crank extractor**
- **10mm Allen key for Shimano freehubs**
- **Appropriate freewheel remover**
- **Chain whips**

All of these can be bought from well-stocked bike shops or ordered through them.

Usually, the first five of these consist of three double-ended spanners, which reduces the bulk of the kit a bit. The best and most expensive of these tools are those made by Campagnolo, Var, Park and Shimano. These are pro quality tools, and are probably overkill for a one-person home workshop, but if you're setting up a club tool kit which will be used by lots of people, then they are a worthwhile investment. For a home workshop, look for the cheaper, but still reasonable quality, tools from Tacx and Madison, who also do peg and lockring spanners which are adjustable for a wide range of bikes. Although the Campagnolo patterns are standard on the more expensive mountain bikes, and up, odd lockring and adjustable cup spanner sizes are sometimes found on cheaper and older bikes. In a club workshop, therefore, adjustable tools for these parts are useful.

Make sure that you get the right headset spanners for your bike. Road-size headsets, usually referred to as one-inch headsets because of the size of steering column on the forks, need 32mm spanners, and are still found on some manufacturer's mountain bikes. Tioga size headsets (1⅛ inch) need 36mm spanners and Fisher Evolution size (1¼ inch) need 40mm spanners. The latter two sizes are referred to as 'oversize' since they are larger than the standard one-inch road bike size which was universally used on mountain bikes before 1989. The two oversize types have the advantages of longer life and greater strength, and the disadvantage of adding four more spanners to an already crowded tool kit.

Good, thin cone spanners are essential, and are not prohibitively expensive. You need a minimum of two 13/14mm spanners and two 15/16mm ones. In addition a 17mm spanner for Shimano lock-nuts is useful, but it does not need to be a dedicated cone spanner.

Your crank extractor should be the same brand as your cranks, to ensure that it fits properly. Alternatively a double-ended extractor such as Park's works on almost all Japanese and Italian cranks and will fit TA cranksets should you ever run across them.

There are two systems of attaching freewheels currently in common use, and they require different tools. Almost all Shimano-equipped bikes use the company's freehub system, where the freewheel body slots on to the hub, is held in place with an internal 10mm Allen key bolt and so needs a 10mm Allen key to remove it. Other freewheels screw on to the hub, and a special tool which fits into the notches or splines in the centre of the freewheel body is needed to remove them. I use a Cyclo tool which is double-ended to fit both SunTour and Shimano freewheels. Every other freewheel manufacturer makes its own remover; most of them are different and a complete set of freewheel removers runs to about a dozen tools. Fortunately, most bikes have SunTour or Shimano freewheels, or clones thereof, and it is unlikely you will ever need any remover but these two. If you do, take your wheel down the bike shop and get the staff to order you the right remover.

Chain whips are not part of some bizarre sado-masochistic bike mechanic's flagellation equipment, but are used to remove sprockets from freewheel bodies, since they usually wear out first. Cyclo make basic ones that are OK for dismantling new blocks, and for holding Shimano Hyperglide blocks while you undo the lockring which holds them onto the freehub body, but for dismantling stubborn blocks better quality units like Tacx and SunTour are more reliable. Eventually most pro mechanics end up making their own chain whips after they've broken a couple of sets on an extremely tight block. One of our mechanics got so fed up with breaking good chain whips that he ran up a set with two-feet long handles made from stainless angle iron and industrial strength rivets holding the chain. They worked.

Advanced tools

This is a small set and contains what *Bicycling* magazine once called the most dangerous tool known to man. We're talking about a spoke key, which in inexpert hands can do more costly damage in less time than anything else in the tool kit.

The advanced tool kit contains the tools you need to true, repair and build wheels. This is a set of jobs which many riders prefer to leave to the wheel wizard at the local bike shop, but if you can true your own wheels they'll last longer. Some people find that they just don't have the patience, and that's a point of view that I can sympathise with; I true my own wheels when I have to, not out of choice. I'd rather be out riding than sitting at a wheel jig, but when there's no option but to true my own wheels I'm glad that I can.

The tools you need are:

- **Wheel truing stand**
- **Spoke key**
- **Wheel dishing tool**

A good wheel truing stand makes the job so much easier that it must be considered essential if you've no experience with wheels. This is a bit of a paradox, because it is not a cheap tool. Before taking the plunge,

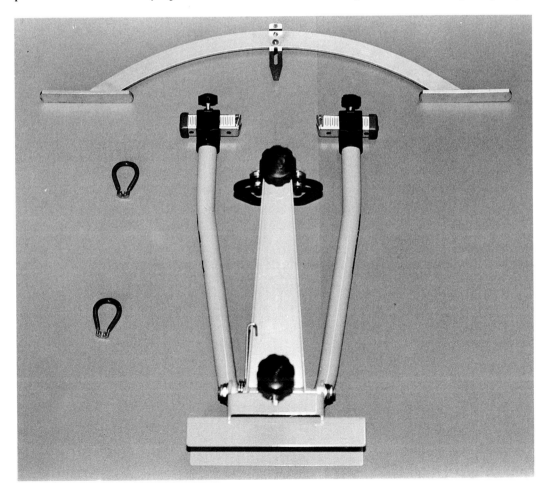

A wheel jig, dishing tool and spoke keys will let you build and maintain your own wheels

see if you can borrow one; if you find you can't stand truing wheels, you haven't wasted any money. It is possible to use a bike frame as a rudimentary wheel stand, but it's less than ideal. A real wheel jig holds the thing securely and at the right height.

Get the best spoke key you can lay your hands on, like a Park, Var or Spokey unit. There are two common sizes of spoke nipple on mountain bikes, British and Japanese; make sure you buy the right one. A spoke key should fit the nipple tightly.

A wheel dishing tool is necessary with most wheel jigs to correctly centre the rim on a rear hub, though the Park jig I use has a centring function designed in and therefore removes the need for a separate dishing tool.

Professional tools

The only pro-level tool which is used in this book is a headset press, and it is only there because it is an example of a job which is virtually impossible to do right without the correct tool. In this case the correct tool costs more than several new headsets, and no-one in their right mind would buy one for home use; headsets just don't need replacing often enough to justify the initial cost, unless you are certain that your children and grandchildren are going to be keen mountain bikers in which case you can always leave it to them in your will.

Other pro-level tools are generally metal-working tools such as thread cutters (taps and dies), reamers, files and so on. If you are

A headset press, for pro use only; they're very good for that one job, but few people could justify the cost

18

already a skilled metalworker, then you may find occasional use for these tools while working on your bike, but in the hands of a novice they are more likely to do harm than good.

Trail tools

There are riders whose trail tool kit consists of nothing but a large dose of optimism. Faced with a wobbly component, miles from help, not having a tool kit will mean a long walk home. Whilst you could carry *all* the tools in your kit everywhere, there are a few that can safely be left behind. Here's what I carry every time I go off road.

- 2,4,5,6mm Allen keys
- 2 x 10mm combination spanner
- Chain splitter
- Spoke key
- Zip ties
- Spare 5mm, 6mm Allen bolts and nuts
- Cone spanners, with one end ground out to fit headset
- Spare tube
- Puncture repair kit
- Presta/Schrader valve adaptor
- Pump

For extended trail rides, see Chapter 15.

Keep your trail tool kit in a seatpack

The workshop

All you really need is enough space to work in, a table to clamp a wheel stand to and a toolbox or two to keep everything in. I usually take over a corner of the MBUK offices when I need to work on my bike, which has the added benefit of being warm. This set-up has the advantage that it can all be packed away neatly when I've finished, but the ideal situation is a permanent workshop. If you can afford to give over an entire room or garage to be a bike workshop, then you end up with a place where you always know where everything is, and you don't have to rummage through the entire tool box looking for that 2mm Allen key because it's on its hook on the tool board.

Of course as soon as your friends get wind of this, they'll be round all the time to fix their bikes. The last time I lived in a house with a dedicated bike workshop it contained six people and twenty bikes. We were running two clubs and a racing team between us, and there was a fairly constant throughput of club members fixing their bikes. We had to keep a close eye on the tools; it's not that people will deliberately walk off with them, just that it's easy to absentmindedly put an Allen key in your pocket when you've finished with it. If you find yourself with this problem paint all your tools an easily recognisable colour, or get them stamped with your initials.

The tool board

Having a dedicated workshop means that you can add a further tool to your kit, a tool board. This is simply a slab of chipboard, say about one by two metres, screwed to the wall, with enough hooks, nails and blocks of wood with holes drilled in them to hold all your tools. When you've found a place for everything, drawing round each item in indelible marker will make them easier to replace.

The importance of having the right tools cannot be over-emphasised. Making do with a pair of pliers and a cheap adjustable spanner is a sure way to strip threads, round nuts and generally do expensive damage. The right tools make the job so much easier that they are a good investment just in terms of reducing hassle and frustration.

3: Cleaning

Everyone remembers their first mountain bike. After every ride, you clean and polish it until it looks like new, recoiling in horror from a small scratch on the top tube. The fact is that you don't have to keep your frame tubes bright and sparkly to make your bike ride better, but it is essential to ensure that the moving parts – brakes, gears, chainset, wheels and so on – are clean. Apart from anything else, it's impossible to perform any maintenance on your bike if it's inches deep in soil samples.

Last summer, I was in a group of about fifteen mountain bikers who spent a week crashing around the Costa Brava. I'd gone to Spain more for the sun and Sangria than the cycling, so took only my basic 'get-me-home' tool kit. But one member of our party went to the extraordinary lengths of bringing with him a bucket, several cans of Jizer cleaning fluid, a hosepipe and piles of rags. We would sit in the bar, drinking the local lager and laughing at Michael, who would be outside polishing his rear mech. After racing each other up and down the beach all week, his bike was fresh as a daisy, whereas mine was looking, and sounding, distinctly the worse for wear.

It makes sense to keep your bike clean. Proper cleaning will help you prolong the life of your bike: done wrongly, it can do more damage than leaving it dirty. Other chapters in this book deal with how to clean specific parts of your bike; what we deal with here is the routine cleaning you should do after every grubby off-road ride.

How much do I have to do?

A mountain bike is designed to be ridden, not put on show in an art gallery. How much time you spend cleaning your bike is a personal thing; I regard time spent polishing up paintwork when I could be out riding as time wasted, but if you're not happy riding unless you've restored your bike to its showroom condition, fine.

So the maximum is up to you: the minimum is to clean and lubricate the chain after every off-road ride. A dirty chain is inefficient: it causes slow gear changes and increases wear on chainrings and sprockets.

Hosing

With the increasing availability of jetwashes, those high pressure hoses usually found at petrol stations, you can clean your bike by putting a coin in the slot and blasting your mud-crusted machine with hot soapy water. Jetwashes are great at shifting even the hardest mud and any other farmyard nasties

Clean the sprockets with the jetwash whilst spinning the pedals to remove accumulated trail debris

that may have attached themselves to your bike, but there are better – if more time-consuming – ways of cleaning your bike. Because jetwashing is so quick and seemingly effective, you may be tempted not to probe any further. Also, in the hands of an inexperienced user, a jetwash can be a dangerous weapon. Most mud usually congregates around the rear sprockets and chainset, so your hosing will be concentrated in these areas, flooding the hub and bottom bracket bearings. The high pressure that those hoses generate is far more than most bearing seals are meant to cope with, and you can end up forcing a lot of water through the seals.

If you really have to use a jetwash, make sure you spray the water away from the bearings. This means, for example, cleaning the chainset by applying the water from the left. Of course, if you're going to remove the bearings and service them anyway, you don't need to be so careful.

Bucket and brush

A far safer, and cheaper, method of cleaning your bike, which ensures that the water goes only where you want it to, is to use a bucket of warm soapy water and a stiff-bristled brush. If you're just cleaning the bike after a ride, there's no need to start removing wheels and chainsets to get to all the little fiddly bits, and if you do it correctly and

Don't spray water directly into the bearings – the seals aren't designed to keep out such a high-pressure spray

thoroughly, you can completely clean the mud from your bike. If you're going to strip down various components, there's no reason not to dismantle your bike and clean them individually.

Start by giving the whole bike a good scrubbing from the top down, cleaning any debris off the tyres and brakes, before working down to the chainset and drive-train. Once the large amount of superficial dirt has been removed, you can concentrate on cleaning the individual parts properly.

Cleaning with solvents

Using a 1 inch paintbrush dipped in a degreasing solution (biodegradable please!), you can clean the heavily gunked up parts of the bike without transferring too much of the dirt to your person. Give the chain a quick clean, then spend a little more time getting the dirt off the front and rear mechs and sprockets. Pay particular attention to the parallelograms that operate the gear mechanisms. Once the pivots of these get greased up, they slow down your gear shifts, and require more force at the thumbshifters. If they get too stiff, they can adversely affect your shifting. Once they're clean, give the chain a proper going over to remove all the muck.

Brakes don't get gunked up to the same extent as the drive-train. After releasing the quick-release cables so that they spring open, give them a good scrubbing, checking the brake-blocks for any small bits of grit which could scour holes in your rims. Then it's on to the saddle and seatpost; scrub them well before finishing off at the handlebars. Now

rinse the whole bike with a bucket of clean water to remove any traces of degreaser.

Sprockets

If the brush is stiff enough, you can usually remove much of the gunge which forms between the sprockets. If you want to get them really clean, don't use too much degreasing solution on them as it will inevitably seep into the hub and freewheel bearings, robbing them of lubricant. Special C-shaped brushes are available to clean this hard-to-reach area, but you can use strips of rag, about 4 inches wide and a foot long, folded over lengthways to form a smooth

edge. This will remove the greasy residue from the sprockets. With the rag or brush in the gap between two sprockets, alternately slide it left and right in the gap, cleaning out the rubbish and spinning the block to move onto the next section.

Chain

The paintbrush should have removed most of the mud, but if your chain is very dirty, it's best to remove it and let it soak in a bucket of cleaner before rinsing, relubricating and refitting. Unfortunately, most chains don't like being taken apart after every ride, so for routine cleaning it's best to

A C-shaped brush makes freewheel
cleaning easy

Drive water out with WD40

leave the chain on the bike. Cleaning chains is a mucky job, but there are chain-cleaning units available consisting of a series of rollers with brushes, which scrub the chain with cleaner, removing all the grit and excess oil. Cleaning the chain by simply running it through a rag in your hand only results in polishing the outer plates, not the inside of the links where it's important. Depending on the degreaser you're using, you may or may not need to rinse the chain; check the bottle for details. Relubricate with a lubricant suitable for mountain bike use such as SuperSpray Lube, Green Mountain, Pedros SynLube or GT85.

Gears

It's important to relubricate the gears after they've been cleaned, because if the pivots are allowed to dry out, they'll be harder to operate than if they were simply dirty. The problem here is to use enough oil to give reasonable penetration and lubrication without flooding the mech and giving dirt

Lubricate just the areas you need to – you'll save money on oil and pick up less dirt

something to stick to. Spray the pivots and springs directly rather than blindly spraying the whole mech with oil; it's more economical on oil anyway.

Brakes

A quick spray with a light lubricant will keep the cantilevers turning on their pivots. Quick-release the brakes, by pulling the cable nipple out of its slot in the arm, and shield the rim with your free hand when spraying with lubricant. After a wet ride it's a good idea to relubricate the cables. Slotted cable stops make this easy, continuous cables don't. Quick-release the brakes, then slide cable housings out of their stops in the frame. The inner cable can now pull out of the slot, to allow you to slide the housings away from their normal position. Get a blob

of grease on the end of your finger, pinch the cable between your finger tips, and rub the grease onto the cable. Now you can slide the housing back into position. When you've done both lengths of outer cable, reconnect the quick-release.

Need to do more?

This is all you'll need to do after most rides, but if you've let your bike get particularly dirty, you may need to service a part more carefully. Often hubs and headsets may need more detailed maintenance, and bottom brackets are susceptible to damp and muck, being close to the ground and directly in line from front-wheel spray. Check the relevant chapters for individual parts.

4: Tyres, tubes and punctures

The variety of tyres available for mountain bikes now is vast and bewildering, but the one thing that all of them have in common is that sooner or later they will puncture. Even the best puncture-resistant tyres, which have kevlar belts under the tread to stop thorns or other debris from penetrating through to the tube, are susceptible to impact punctures, so fixing a puncture is probably the most basic skill a cyclist needs.

That said, there are mountain bikers who lead an utterly charmed life and just don't get punctures. Australian mountain bike champion Tony Smith turned up in Britain a couple of years ago, on his way to the World Championships in Switzerland, and took in a round of the Shimano Series (the first British Championship series) which I was organising. Tony rode the two hundred miles to the race venue, raced, then spent the next few weeks riding round Britain, then on to Switzerland, all without a single puncture. Good job too, since we later found out that he didn't know how to fix one! Unfortunately, come the Worlds, Tony got fairly badly knocked about when he crashed after puncturing, and had a long walk back down the mountain to the finish line.

Ask most bike shop mechanics to repair a punctured inner tube for you and you'll get a funny look, with usually a straight refusal.

Patching a tube just isn't worth the effort; at their hourly rates it's cheaper to fit a new tube than try to repair the old one.

The same is true of fixing a flat on the trail. There's absolutely no point trying to repair a tube if it's wet and cold, and even if it's fine, you don't want to hold everyone up while you wait for the glue to set. No, the thing to do is to carry a spare tube, and replace the punctured tube with a fresh one. Fix the punctured tube when you get home.

This sounds pretty obvious, but there are some techniques that will speed up the process. These are especially useful to racers, but recreational riders can also benefit from fast tube replacement; who wants to spend time fixing a tyre when they could be riding?

Changing tyres

The secret of fast tube changes is to carefully match tyres and rims. I use Mavic M6CD rims for fun and recreational riding. At 490g each, they're by no means the lightest rims around, but they have two big advantages; they're tough, and their deep shape means that tyres come off them really easily. Racing on M6CDs, '89 National Champion Deb Murrell astonished spectators by pulling her punctured back wheel out of her bike and ripping the tyre off with her bare hands.

Easy, if you know how, and the way how is to use M6CDs or another rim that allows quick tyre removal. This list includes Mavic Energy M7, Araya RM-17, Campagnolo Thorr and Contax and most other rims that have a deep well.

Choice of tyre is important, too: some will come off easily, some need tools. If your choice of tyres is down to a few, then take a wheel into the shop and select the tyre that most easily comes off your rims.

I also use slightly undersized inner tubes, so that the tube doesn't impede tyre fitting or removal. 1.5inch butyl or latex tubes stretch quite happily to fit 2inch tyres. Polyurethane tubes, however, don't stretch and must be sized accurately.

To fix a flat fast, all you need if you've chosen tyres and rims carefully is a pump or gas canisters and a spare tube. I carry 1.5in Presta tubes as spares, so that I can lend a spare to anyone else who punctures; Presta valves will fit through a rim that's drilled for Schrader, but a fat Schrader tube won't go through a Presta-sized hole. Some tyre/rim combinations allow you to literally just pull the tyre off the side of the rim. If the tyre is a very tight fit you'll need tyre levers; more of this later.

Removing the wheel

Most mountain bikes nowadays come with quick release wheels. It can still be awkward to get a fully inflated tyre through a brake, but since we're talking about a flat tyre here, that's not a problem. If it's a rear wheel, put the gear on to the smallest sprocket, open the quick release, pull the mechanism back out of the way and drop the tyre out. Front wheels just drop out of the fork, unless you've got 'safety drop-outs' which have a ridge to stop a flipped-open quick release

wheel from falling out while you're riding. You'll have to unscrew the quick release lever a few turns to get the wheel to drop out, making it into a slow release. Racers tend to choose forks without safety drop-outs, or grind them off; when you're in a hurry they're a pain. However, they can be a life-saver if your preparation is not meticulous, or if you're unfortunate enough to have a front QR flip open. A few years ago I was riding through the woods, on some pretty serious downhills, when I noticed the front end of my borrowed Rockhopper was vibrating under braking. I assumed it was a loose headset, and pulled up to wait for the rest of the group, in the hope that someone would be carrying a headset spanner. On closer inspection I discovered that I had an

Releasing the front quick-release. Make sure you fasten it securely when you've finished

open front QR and the only thing keeping my front wheel in place was a pair of axle retainers.

Removing the tyres

Most tyres are somewhere between a slack and a tight fit. To remove one of these, first let all the air out of the tyre. For a slow puncture this will mean opening the valve and squeezing the tyre to expel the last of the air. Presta valves are opened by unscrewing the top part of the valve and pushing it down, Schrader by pushing the centre of the valve.

Next, push the bead away from the edge of the rim, into the well, right round the circumference of the rim. This liberates all the slack that's available. Grab the sidewall between both fingers and thumbs, with your hands about three inches apart. Pull the bead up out of the well and pop it out over the edge of the rim. Gradually work your hands apart, pulling out more and more of the bead until you can just slip your finger under and pull it off the rim.

What caused the puncture?

Pull the inner tube out and run your hands around the inside of the tyre until you find the cause of the puncture. This may be a bit of glass, so don't feel for it too vigorously or you'll cut your fingers. If you can't find the cause, don't worry. If the puncture was very rapid it was almost certainly a 'snakebite' impact puncture. This is caused by the inner tube being pinched between the tyre and rim when the tyre bottoms out against the rim as it hits a rock or other obstacle. Snakebites leave a characteristic double hole in the tube, hence the name, and can be prevented by keeping tyre pressures fairly high, or using the fattest tyres you can fit into your frame.

Impact punctures can be dangerous. A sudden front tyre puncture at high speed usually causes a disastrous loss of control, another good reason for keeping your speed sensible on steep downhills.

If the flat was very slow the cause may be a very fine piece of wire or thorn. I once spent two months replacing tubes every other ride until I finally found the thin wire strand that was causing all the flats.

If you're having this kind of problem, the only ways to cure it are either to replace the tyre, or to spend as-long-as-it-takes going over the tyre with a fine toothcomb until you find the offending object. A bright light helps, as does locating the hole in the inner tube, and thus narrowing down the area of the tyre you need to investigate.

Fitting the inner tube

Partially inflate the new tube, just enough so that it holds its shape (experienced riders, and those in a mega-race-type hurry, can omit this step, but it does help prevent the tube from getting pinched by the tyre). Put the valve through the valve hole and put the tube into the tyre. Push the tyre over the rim so that the bead sits next to the sidewall. Starting from the valve, lift the bead over the sidewall and push it down into the well, pulling the slack round the rim as you go. Make sure the valve is pushed well into the tyre so that the area by the valve doesn't puncture.

The last few inches are the hardest. Work them on gradually by gripping the body of the tyre and pulling the beads on with your thumbs. This takes practice, but you should be able to fit even the tightest tyres without recourse to tyre levers.

Partially inflate the inner tube to avoid pinching on replacement

Using tyre levers

Very tight rim/tyre combos will require tyre levers to get them off. The right way to use tyre levers is to slip two under the bead, four to eight inches apart, next to spokes, then lift the bead over the rim and hook the levers onto the spokes. If you put one lever in and hook it to the spoke it will pull the bead so tight that it'll be very difficult to get the next lever in.

You may need to unhook one lever and work it round the rim to free the rest of the tyre. To replace the tube, proceed as above.

Put the wheel back in the frame before inflating the tyre. This saves you the hassle of opening the brake.

Inflating the tube

Racers use gas canisters, the rest of us carry pumps. Some puncture kits come with rather small gas canisters, but there are now huge 25g Air Zefal cartridges available.

When removing a tight-fitting tyre with tyre levers push the tyre lever around rather than prising the tyre off the rim

These will get a 2 inch tyre up to full pressure in seconds, but they're a fairly expensive way of fixing a flat – worth it for racers, but probably a bit over the top for casual riding. My favourite pump is still the Mt Zefal Plus. I've lost them, but I don't know anyone who's managed to break one or wear one out yet.

Puncture repair

Puncture repair kits have improved to the point where a good puncture repair can be regarded as permanent, so it's worth fixing the tube.

Stuff the dead tube in your tool bag or jersey pocket, and fix it when you get home. You need a puncture repair kit like the Tip Top or Nutrak ones. Here's how:

1 Locating the puncture

Having removed the tube from the tyre, pump it up so that it is about 2 inches across. If you're using a track pump, go carefully; it's quite easy to completely destroy a tube by over-inflating it until it explodes, and I know people who've done this while chatting away as they inflated a tube. Saves fixing it, I suppose.

To find the hole, pass the inflated tube near to your face and listen for the hiss of escaping air. If this doesn't work, the hole is very small and the way to find it is to minutely inspect the tyre by eye. Eventually you'll find the hole by getting a thin jet of air in your eye, though this can take some time.

The foolproof way of hunting for a hole in a tube is by passing it through water, but this has the disadvantage that it leaves the tube wet, and you've then got to dry it before you can fix it. However, it is a useful last resort when searching for the tiny pinholes that cause maddening slow punctures.

2 Preparing the tube for repair

Mark the hole by roughening the area around it with the emery cloth or sandpaper from the puncture repair kit. Deflate the tube. Roughen an area of the tube just bigger than the patch – this is an essential step because it vastly increases the ease with which the patch can stick to the tube. Spread a thin layer of glue over the roughened area.The glue needs to be practically dry before you apply the patch, so give it a few minutes to get tacky.

3 Fitting the patch

Peel the backing off the patch (the silver foil not the clear plastic) and press it firmly on the hole. If I've got the time, I usually put the tube under a pile of books to hold the patch on firmly while it sets. Give it at least several minutes to set, then inflate the tube gently to test the seal and leave it for an hour or so, so you can tell whether it's going down. Don't inflate it humungously hard; if you pump it up to above its normal inflated size, you can blow off even the best patch.

Choosing tubes and tyres

There is a huge range of tyres on the market, and several different types of inner tubes to go inside them. It's not possible to give details of them all here, not least because by the time this book appears there will probably be a dozen new ones on the market which I don't know about yet!

The simplest choice is of inner tube. Broadly there are three types, standard butyl rubber, which is black and is the most common by

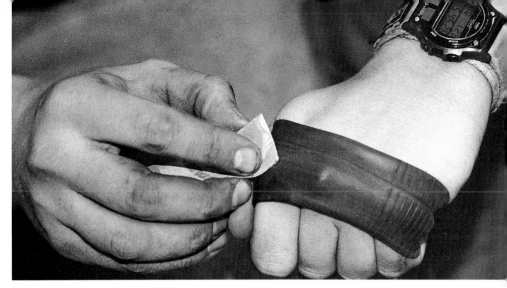
Roughening an inner tube prior to glueing

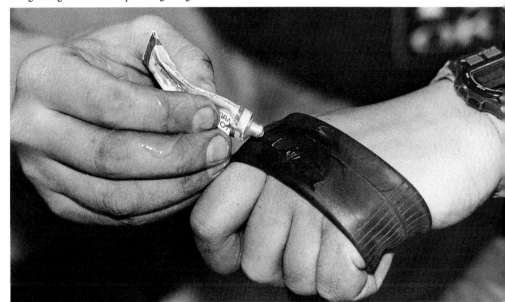
Applying the glue

Fitting the patch

far, natural latex rubber, usually coloured blue or pink, and polyurethane, which is nearly clear in colour and much stiffer than the other two.

Butyl tubes have the advantage of being cheap, very widely available and fairly easily reparable. I like Michelin's 1.5in butyl tubes, which are of consistently good quality and fairly light.

Check the length of the valve if you are using narrow, deep rims; some valves do not leave enough shaft protruding from the rim, making them impossible to pump up.

Latex tubes are a relatively recent innovation in mountain bikes, though roadies have been using them for years. Latex is much more flexible than butyl rubber so it tends to give rather than tear when confronted with a sharp object and this makes latex tubes more puncture-resistant than butyl ones. Because most puncture repair kits contain glue that is intended to work on natural rubber rather than butyl, latex tubes are somewhat easier to repair than other types. Latex tubes tend to be a bit oversized, so it is sensible to use the smallest ones you can find.

More recently polyurethane tubes have become available. The toughness of the material helps reduce punctures, but they are hard to fix when they *do* puncture and a special repair kit is needed. They are usually lighter than butyl tubes, but must be an exact fit in the tyre, because they don't stretch much when inflated. This can make them awkward to fit. (To say the least. I once spent half an hour trying to wrestle a polyurethane tube into a tyre that it was supposed to fit, before giving up in disgust and using a butyl tube!)

Choice of tyre depends on a number of factors including the type of surface you usually ride on, your weight, your riding style and how much you are prepared to risk reliability for speed if you're racing.

One complication of choosing tyres is that the markings on tyre sidewalls do not accurately reflect the size of the tyre. A batch of tyres from different manufacturers, all marked 26 x 2.0, will differ by as much as 6mm in the actual width and depth of the tyre. Since it is the width and therefore the air volume of the tyre that determines how well it will cushion the rim and rider, it would be useful for this information to be accurate. There are moves afoot among tyre manufacturers to introduce a standard system of markings which will give the tyre's actual width in millimetres. For the moment, however, you may as well disregard the sidewall measurements and go on how fat the tyre looks – it's about as accurate.

The thinnest off road tyre currently available is Specialized's 1.5in *Hardpack*. This is useful for very light, smooth racers on relatively smooth courses with no significant high-speed descents, but does not really provide enough protection from impact punctures at sensible pressures for it to have many other applications. The fattest rubber is the 2.5in *Ground Control Extreme*, also from Specialized, which provides outstanding traction and cushioning, but is a little heavy for many riders' tastes. In between is a huge range.

It goes without saying that the thinner tyres, usually nominally 1.9in wide, will be lighter and therefore accelerate and climb better. However, the problem with such tyres is that they are prone to bottoming out and developing impact punctures, unless you keep them pumped up fairly hard. This in turn reduces traction and comfort, and is really only a practical compromise if you're racing, and you're fairly light. Most riders use slightly larger tyres, nominally 1.95, 2.0 or 2.1 inches, and good brands to look out for include Specialized, Onza, Ritchey, Tioga, Kona, Marin, Panaracer and Michelin.

All these manufacturers have their own ideas about tread patterns, but there are some general principles that apply to all tyres. The tread of a tyre basically consists of two areas: the centre, which is in contact with the ground when the bike is going in a straight line; and the edges, which come into play in cornering. Widely-spaced treads work well in mud, while tighter treads are better in sandy soils and on dry, hard-packed dirt. Tall, well-supported side lugs give good cornering, though if they are too tall they will fold and the tyre will slide.

Tread compound makes a difference to tyre performance, especially in the wet, as well as to durability, and manufacturers are always trying to balance grip and longevity. The ultimate high-traction tyres were the limited run of white rubber Onza Porcupines which were briefly manufactured in mid-1990 for downhill racing, but the tread compound was so soft that they had to be replaced after a few races. This sort of design is clearly not practical for most riders, whose wallets will not run to frequent tyre replacement, so most manufacturers use tread compounds that afford less traction but better durability. Soft-treaded tyres like standard Onza Porcupines and Panaracer Smokes are superb off road, but tend to wear quickly if used on tarmac. More durable tread compounds are used by Specialized and Ritchey, whose tyres are more suitable for multi-purpose use. Hardcore riders and racers may have several different types of tyres for different terrain, but equally many riders use the same tyres no matter what. One thing is for certain; you don't have to stick with the same kind of rubber that your bike came fitted with.

The best source of information as to which tyres work well in your area is your local enthusiast mountain bike shop; a bike shop staffed by mountain bikers is an invaluable resource.

5: Transmission

The transmission, which consists of the chainrings, gears and chain of your mountain bike, is the most complicated single system on the machine and also accounts for the largest number of moving parts on any bike. Transmission parts are relatively expensive and tend to wear out much more quickly if not kept clean and well-lubricated. The most important component of the transmission is the chain.

Mountain bike chains have a ridiculously hard life. We expect them to transmit pedalling effort, shift easily from sprocket to sprocket when we want them to, but stay put when we don't, last forever, and do all this while covered in highly abrasive dirt.

Well, the good news is that, by and large, chains work incredibly well, especially if they get the right sort of tender loving care and you're careful about little things like splitting and joining them.

The chain

Because the chain is far and away the most exposed of the bike's moving parts, it picks up more grime than any other. This grime contains silica, the basic mineral from which rock and soil are formed.

Silica particles are considerably harder than steel bike chains, so tiny particles of it in the links of the chain act as grinding paste, wearing away the bearing surfaces. After a period of time this wear, accumulated over all the links of the chain, combined with a slight elongation of the side plates, causes the chain to become longer.

Sprockets and chainrings are designed to be used with chains that have their rollers exactly half an inch apart, and such chains are referred to as half-inch pitch for this reason. There are advantages to smaller pitch chains, such as the 10mm pitch system Shimano attempted to introduce for track and road bikes a few years ago, but the half-inch pitch is now so entrenched that it will remain long after everything else in bicycles has gone metric. No-one will ever talk about 12.7mm chains!

Anyway, the point we're getting to here is that a worn chain has rollers spaced fractionally more than a half-inch apart. This means that all the load on the chain goes through one roller and one sprocket and chainring tooth at a time, rather than being spread over several of each. This accelerates wear on the sprocket and chainring teeth, causing them to become hooked and eventually so worn that a new chain slips over them and the whole bang-shoot, sprockets, chain and rings, needs replacing at once. This is an expensive business and can be delayed by diligent chain maintenance; if you don't clean anything else on your mountain bike, you should at least clean the chain.

Cleaning and lubrication

Most riders hose their bikes down after a ride; keep the water away from the hub, bottom bracket and headset bearings and this works fine. Hosing is probably the best way of shifting superficial mud from the chain and getting it clean enough so you can clean it properly, or in other words removing enough of the coarse mud off the top to get at the fine stuff underneath.

The fiddly way to clean a chain is to split it, take it off the bike and soak it in solvent. This is possible for most chains (see *Removing the chain* page 38) but the narrow chains on all Shimano Hyperglide-equipped bikes are not amenable to this kind of treatment, for reasons that will become apparent later.

A Hyperglide chain needs to be cleaned in

Cleaning the chain with a Park chain cleaner is much easier than removing the chain and using solvent

situ and this is best done either by scrubbing it with a stiff paintbrush, then an old toothbrush, and solvent such as diesel, or Cyclon or Madison chain cleaner, or by running it through a Park or Vetta chain cleaner, a plastic solvent bath which clamps round the chain and runs it through solvent and between brushes which scrub out the grime. A really grubby chain will take a few goes through one of these devices to get it properly clean, with fresh solvent each time. This is the easiest way to clean any chain.

After you've got it clean, lubricate it with a thick spray oil such as Super Spray Lube MTB, Rockoil or Madison Ultra Lube. The easiest way to lubricate it is to hold the spray can still and turn the pedals quickly backwards to pass the chain by the lubricant spray. Sounds obvious, I know, but I have seen people use a whole can of lube in one go, trying to pass the can along the chain and get into the fiddly bits around the rear mech and chainset.

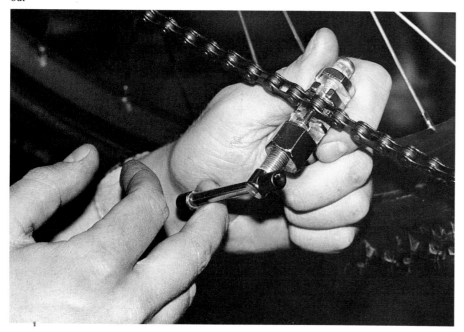

Removing a chain with a chain splitter. Take care not to push the pin all the way out

Removing the chain

A chain needs replacing when twelve full links measure 12⅛ inches long. Any longer and there will be wear on the sprockets and chainrings as well, necessitating their replacement.

If the chain is slipping on the sprockets or chainrings, then it is way past time it was replaced and you'll need new chainrings and sprockets as well. I recently acquired a Trek bike that had done a 5,000 mile expedition and the transmission was completely shot because the rider, reasoning that chains are heavy things to carry as spares, had simply not bothered to replace it when it got worn. The middle ring was completely shot, and the cassette and chain also needed replacing: the total bill was nearly three times the price of a replacement chain.

To replace the chain you first have to get it off, and of course you might want to remove it to clean it. To do this, you need a chain splitting tool, as sold in bike shops everywhere. A chain splitter has two sets of locating ridges for the chain. The one furthest away from the punch is for splitting and rejoining it, and the other nearer the punch is for adjusting a stiff link.

I still hear of people asking for split links for derailleur geared bikes, but unfortunately, although they do exist, they don't work. The kind of split link which old three-speeds used to have, which you prise open with a screwdriver, will spontaneously prise itself open as it passes through the jockey wheels of a derailleur, and so can't be used. To break a derailleur chain, you need a chain splitter.

Place the chain on the splitting and joining ridge and turn the handle to screw the punch into the chain and partially push out the pin. Don't drive the pin all the way through,

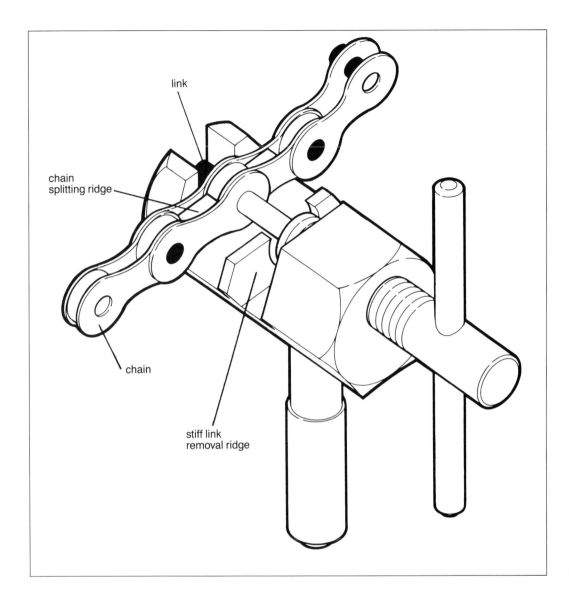

link

chain
splitting ridge

chain

stiff link
removal ridge

Chain splitter

push it out so that it is retained in the outside plate. Trying to replace a pin in a chain once it has been pushed out all the way is possible but extremely difficult. If necessary, back the punch off and try to part the chain after each turn until it will separate.

With the chain separated, pull it through the front and rear mechs to finally take it off the bike. To clean it, dump it in a tin of solvent and leave it to soak for half an hour, then if you're using Cyclon chain cleaner, rinse out the solvent under the tap and hang it up to dry. Lubricate as above and hang it up so the excess lube can drip off.

Fitting the chain

To refit the old chain, position it on the splitting and joining links and push the pin back into the chain. To fit a new chain you

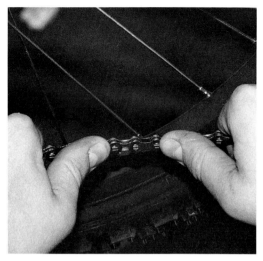

A stiff link shows up when the chain clicks once a revolution for no apparent reason

Curing a stiff link

first need to trim it to the same length as the old one. To do this, lay the two chains out so that they start at the same place and measure the required length of the new chain off against the old chain. Hyperglide chains should only be trimmed at the end which does not have a pin sticking out of it.

Thread the chain through the gears and rejoin it. If rejoining the chain produces a stiff link, which will click as it goes through the gears, it can be cured by pushing the pin through or back a fraction with the stiff link removal plates or by simple brute force; grab the chain either side of the stiff link with your fingers and thumbs and flex it from side to side.

Hyperglide chains

These chains are found on almost all Shimano-equipped bikes since 1989. They are joined by a special black link which has oversized ends. This link should not be used to split the chain. An HG chain can be split anywhere except at the joining pin, which has oversized ends and will damage the chain as it comes out.

A new HG chain must be joined with the pin which comes fitted to its open end, so don't take this off when trimming it. Shimano make special pins for rejoining HG chains, which are available from Shimano Service Dealers. The old pin should be pushed right out and the new pin, which has an extended pointed end to locate it in the chain, used in its place. The extended end should then be broken off with pliers.

All of this is necessary because HG chains have the links peened over to prevent them coming apart under the strain of normal use, but paradoxically this creates problems when you actually want to take them apart. As you push out the pin it leaves a large hole in the plate which does not properly hold the pin when it's refitted. Consequently, the chain spontaneously parts when you're out riding. I had a Hyperglide chain which had not been joined properly (I installed it before Shimano realised they had a problem with this design) and it was coming apart with monotonous regularity. I reached the point where I didn't go anywhere without a chain splitter, and got very good at recognising the noise the chain made just before it came apart.

The joining pin which the chain comes with, and the special pins which must be used to rejoin the chain, have oversized ends to prevent this problem.

Although this seems on the surface to be a lot of hassle, it is very rare for a properly joined HG chain to come apart in use, and if they are cleaned and maintained well, they are very durable.

The rear derailleur

Most engineers find the humble rear derailleur a pretty offensive device. You see, chains just aren't meant to de-rail; in virtually every other application of a chain as a drive mechanism it sits permanently on two sprockets. If gears are needed they are achieved by systems of gear wheels that are independent of the chain, like those in a motorbike gear box. These systems aren't practical on bicycles because they're heavy, or at least the standard system of derailleurs and multiple sprockets is lighter. In many engineers' eyes, though, the amazing thing about modern derailleurs is not how well they work, but that they work at all!

It is a genuine source of amazement that derailleurs continue to work when covered in a mixture of heather, leafmould, mud and sheep debris, and it's no real surprise when things go wrong, but a little simple cleaning and preventive maintenance will stop most problems before they start.

Cleaning

There are riders who like to go around with a layer of crud on their bikes 'to prove it gets off-road' but they still need an efficient gear-

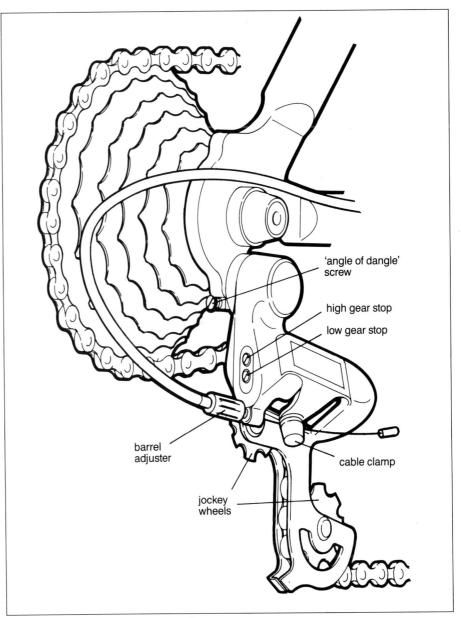

Rear mech

shifting system – and that means a clean one.

Hose the mud off as usual. Clean and lubricate the chain (see pages 24-26) then scrub off any remaining mud with an old toothbrush and solvent.

41

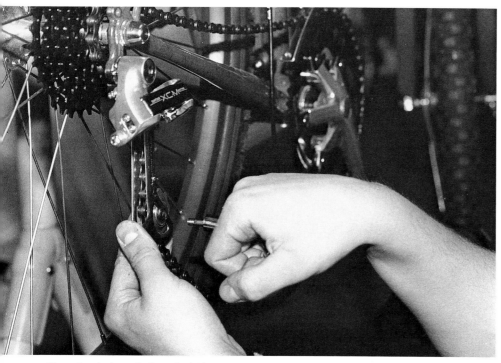

Lubricate all the mech's moving parts; jockey wheels, springs, pivots and cables. Sticky and kinked control cables are a major cause of hassle with indexed gear systems; if in doubt, replace them. Get the original manufacturer's cables if you can, but if not, Clarks make excellent replacement gear cables.

Replacing the mechanism

If you've managed to mangle your rear mech, you'll need to replace it. The rear mech attaches to the frame of most bikes by an Allen key bolt. To remove it, undo the lower jockey wheel to take the mech off the chain (this is to avoid splitting the chain, which is unnecessary hassle for most bikes and should be avoided on Shimano-equipped bikes), undo the cable clamp bolt and unscrew the mech mounting bolt. Reverse the process to fit the new mech.

Removing the lower jockey wheel (above) prior to removing the rear mech

When a rear mech gets written off it can damage something else in the process, usually the chain, which gets twisted, or the gear hanger. A twisted chain is incurable and must be replaced, but a bent gear hanger on a steel frame can be bent back into place. If the gear hanger is bent, the new mech will not hang straight, but will lean towards or away from the spokes. Special tools are available to exactly align a gear hanger, but with practice it can be done with a couple of twelve-inch adjustable spanners, one on the hanger, one on the dropout. The spanner on the hanger is moved gently until the two are in line. This is a technique best left to bike shop mechanics.

Aluminium gear hangers cannot be realigned in this way because aluminium 'work-hardens' when it is bent. This means that it becomes brittle very easily, so is much more fragile after it has been realigned. Cannondale get around this by using a bolt-on gear hanger which can be replaced if it is damaged.

Cable replacement

The cable is attached to the rear mech by an Allen key bolt or a nut, depending on the make and model of derailleur. Virtually all current SunTour and Shimano rear mechs use a 5mm Allen key cable fixing bolt, though some cheaper models use a nut. Undo the bolt or nut. (Almost all bolts, nuts and other threaded components on bikes have standard right-hand threads and therefore unscrew anti-clockwise and screw in, or tighten, clockwise. There are a couple of exceptions, which we'll get to in later chapters.) If there is a cable end cap, pull it off with pliers, and withdraw the cable from the cable outers at the rear mech, shifter and seat cluster if the cable is top routed.

Fill the cable outers with a thin, slippery lubricant, such as Superspray MTB Lube or LPS. The little tube that comes with some brands of lube is very useful for this.

At this point, take a look at the condition of the top jockey wheel. Shimano top jockeys are supposed to have a small amount of side to side movement, but they should move sideways smoothly and not rock around the clamp bolt. SunTour top jockeys are not supposed to move sideways, but experience has shown that SunTour's gear systems often work best when the top jockey has developed a small amount of sloppiness. If the top jockey seems to be excessively worn, replace it. Bear in mind that you should get the manufacturer's own replacement top jockey; SunTour and Shimano jockeys are not interchangeable.

Getting the old cable out of a conventional thumbshifter is easy; just pull it out. Shimano Deore DX and XT Rapid Fire (STI) and SunTour X-Press under-handlebar shifters are more complicated and require partial disassembly to get the cable out.

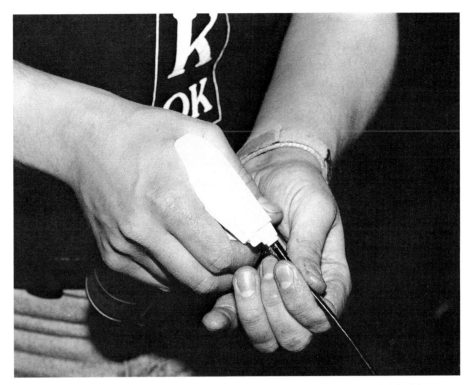

Fill the cable outer with light lube

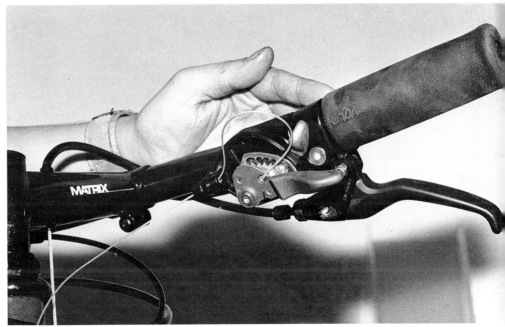

The cable retaining system in a SunTour X-Press shifter with the plastic cover removed

43

SunTour cables are removed by unscrewing the central screw on the underside of the shifter and taking off the cover plate. This is made from fairly soft plastic and can therefore be flexed to get it off the shift levers; it's not unbreakable, though, so be gentle with it. The cable end will now be visible in the metal section which the levers are attached to and can be pulled out.

For some reason SunTour have chosen to use a different shape of cable end from everyone else. Rather than have the cable attach to the end of a cylindrical nipple, SunTour attach it to the side, so you do need a specific SunTour replacement cable.

To remove the cable from Shimano DX or XT Rapid Fire shifter, press the top lever six or more times, so the shifter is in its highest gear position, then remove the small cross-headed screw that is above the small lever and take off the cover plate that it holds on. The cable nipple should be visible under it. If it's not, put the cover plate back on and take the bike to a dealer. Rapid Fire shifters are sufficiently complicated that further disassembly is unwise, to say the least, and best left to expert mechanics. Rapid Fire shifters below DX in the Shimano range have a large hole in the body which the cable can be pushed out of when the shifter is in its highest-gear position. Thread the new cable into the shifter, through the cable outers and guides and into the rear mech.

Cable adjustment

Before you tighten the cable on a new mech you'll need to adjust it; you'll also need to do this if the gears have gone out of adjustment for whatever reason. There are three adjusting screws on a rear mech; these limit the in and out movement of the mech and adjust the tension of the top spring, which in turn affects the angle which the mech hangs at (Shimano call this a 'b-tension adjustment screw' but we tend to call it the 'angle of dangle' screw.) In addition, the

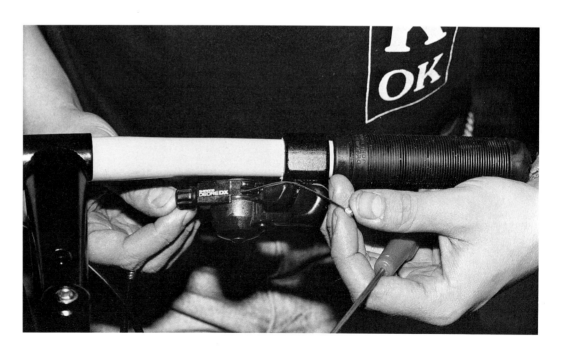

Fitting a cable to a Deore DX STI lever

44

barrel adjuster on the cable outer trims the indexing.

For all rear mechs screw the barrel adjuster all the way in, then out again a couple of turns. Push the mech all the way up to the big sprocket by hand, and use the lower of the two screws on the back of the mech to set it so that it stops on the biggest sprocket and doesn't go into the spokes or stop on a lower sprocket. Turning the screw anti-clockwise allows the mech to move nearer the spokes; turning it clockwise moves the mech away from the spokes.

Allow the mech to spring back to the smallest sprocket and use the top screw to adjust the position of the mech.

The angle of dangle screw is used to adjust the trim of the mech so that the top jockey wheel moves as close as possible to the sprockets for efficient shifting, without rubbing on them. If the top jockey rubs on a sprocket, turn the angle of dangle screw until it doesn't.

If you're just replacing the cable these steps are unnecessary, but you do need to adjust the barrel adjuster to get the indexing right.

Adjusting the end stops on a rear mech. Setting them wrong will mean the chain is thrown off the sprockets, or it won't travel the full width of the block

Pull the cable taut with pliers or a 'fourth-hand' cable puller and tighten the cable anchor bolt. Pull the bare cable at the down tube or top tube sideways by hand to pre-stretch it, and take up any slack that is generated by loosening off the anchor bolt and repeating the last step.

Shift from the smallest to the next smallest sprocket. If this does not happen on the first click of the shifter, unscrew the barrel adjuster until it does.

Exact adjustment of the indexing varies between SunTour and Shimano rear mechs. To set the indexing on a Shimano rear mech, move the shifter to the second smallest sprocket and screw the barrel adjuster out until the chain almost rubs on the third sprocket. For SunTour, set the barrel adjuster so that the chain runs smoothly on the third sprocket. If you're not sure just what the barrel adjuster does, try rotating it a turn from these positions and note the effect on the indexing.

Routine maintenance

After initial setting up, the only adjustment aside from lubrication that a rear gear needs is to take up the slack in the cable. Unscrew the barrel adjuster a little after the cable has had a week or so to bed in.

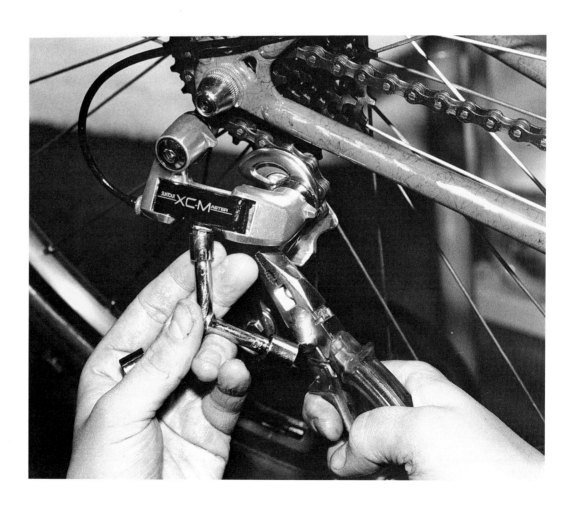

Tighten the cable clamp whilst pulling the slack cable through with a pair of pliers. Anti-clockwise tightens the cable, clockwise slackens

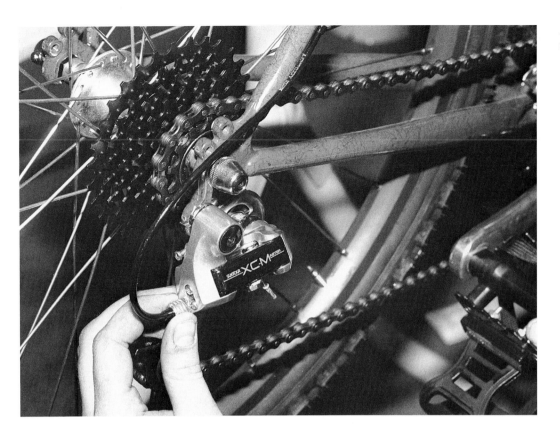

Lubricate the mech and cable frequently. If your bike has slotted cable stops you can get at the inner to lubricate it really easily; put the bike in lowest gear, then move the shifter to its high-gear position to generate slack in the cable. You will now be able to pull the cable out of the stops and wipe lube on to it with a clean, lubricated cloth.

The front derailleur

If engineers find rear gear mechanisms offensive, then front derailleurs can only be described as crude. A front mech simply shoves the chain across from one chainring to another by the unsubtle method of hitting it with a steel plate. Sophisticated it ain't. Nevertheless, front mechs have come a long way from the first designs which appeared in the thirties. The earliest front mechs consisted of two parallel plates that simply pushed the chain sideways from ring to ring. As a result they had a very narrow range, as little as eight or ten teeth, and didn't work spectacularly well. The best modern mountain bike front derailleurs can cope with a total difference between chainrings of 26 teeth, and will shift in pretty appalling conditions. All you really need to do is keep them clean, well-lubricated and well-adjusted.

Cleaning

After you've hosed off the inevitable mud (taking care to keep the water away from the nearby bottom bracket bearings) any well-attached dirt can be scrubbed off with solvent and an old toothbrush.

Front mechs rarely malfunction because they are dirty, but cleaning them allows you to check the condition of their various parts, especially the two plates that form the cage. Eventually most front mechs break, because one of the plates wears out from the continual abrasion of the chain during shifting, and it's worth keeping an eye on the condition of the plates; if they look excessively worn, replace the mech.

Seized mechanisms

Front mechs do malfunction because they have not been kept lubricated, and the simple symptoms of this are that the mech seizes up or becomes very stiff. A very stiff front mech action may also be the result of cable or shifter problems, so to check the cause, disconnect the cable at the mech by undoing the cable clamp bolt, and try to move it by hand. This will require quite a lot of force, since front mechs have strong springs, but it should be possible. If it is not, the mech is seized.

To unseize a front mech, you need to take it off the frame. Undo the frame clamp bolt and the cable clamp bolt, if you haven't already, then take out the little screw which holds the cage plates together. This will allow you to flex the plates far enough apart for the chain to slip between them, and it is less hassle than splitting the chain. Put the cage screw back in, so you can't lose it.

Soak the mech in the thinnest penetrating lubricant you can find, like WD-40, Duck Oil or Super Spray Lube and leave it to creep into the pivots for a few hours. Then attempt to move the cage again. It should now be possible to get the mech to move a little, and repeated applications of penetrating oil and brute force should eventually restore it to full, free mobility. If it

won't free up there's no option but to throw it away and get a new one.

Front cable replacement

If there's nothing wrong with the mech, then any stiffness in the system is the result a sticky cable, and the simplest way to cure the problem is to replace it.

Removing the old cable from a front shifter is much the same as from a rear shifter. For a conventional thumbshifter, just undo the clamp bolt and pull it out of the shifter. To get the cable out of a SunTour X-Press shifter unit, undo the grey cover plate, remove it and pull the cable out of the innards of the shifter. For Shimano STI units from LX down, put the shifter in its low-gear position by pressing the top 'button' twice, and push the cable out of the mech body. DX and XT units have a cover plate just above the top button which must be removed to get the cable out. If the cable won't come out, refer the problem to a dealer; dismantling STI units is a job for experienced mechanics only.

Fill the cable outers with thin lube, thread the cable through them and the frame stops and reconnect the cable to the mech. Put a cable end cap on the cable and crimp it on with pliers.

Fitting the mechanism

Front mechs have four adjustments, angle, position, big ring limit and small ring limit. In addition, indexed front derailleurs need precise adjustment of the cable tension to align them on the middle ring. I've always felt that front indexing was a solution in search of a problem, but both Shimano and Campagnolo seem to think we need it, so we need to know how to tweak it.

Undo the cage screw and slip the mech over the chain. Replace the cage screw and tighten it. (This step is unnecessary if you've taken the chain off, of course.) Undo the clamp bolt and attach the mech loosely to the seat tube.

Some Shimano front mechs, particularly on oversize frames, use an 'endless band' clamp. These are fitted by undoing the Allen key bolt, taking off the clamp and reassembling it around the seat tube.

The front mech should be positioned so that the outer cage plate clears the big ring by about 2mm, when you move the mech up to the big ring position. If you have elliptical rings, the mech should clear the highest point of them by about 2mm. The outer plate should also be parallel to the big ring when viewed from above. With the mech correctly positioned, tighten the clamp bolt. Sometimes a mech will shift position slightly as the clamp bolt is tightened. If this happens, note how much it has moved, loosen it off, move it the same amount in the opposite direction to compensate, then tighten it up.

Adjustment

With the mech now correctly positioned, all that remains is to adjust the limit screws to stop the chain from falling off the big and small rings, connect the cable, and tweak the cable tension so the front indexing, if any, is accurate.

Put the rear mech into the smallest sprocket and push the front mech up to the big ring manually. The outer plate should just clear the chain. If it doesn't, use the big ring limit screw, the outer of the two screws on the top of the mech, to move it in or out as necessary.

Adjusting the travel on a front mech

Let the mech spring back to the little ring and put the rear mech in the largest sprocket. The chain should just clear the inner plate of the front mech. Use the small ring limit screw to adjust it.

You can now attach the cable to the mech. Put the shifter in its low-gear position and pull the cable through the clamp bolt with pliers or a fourth hand tool so that it is just taut. Tighten the clamp bolt.

Check that the front mech now shifts quickly to the big and small rings in all the gears, and especially that it drops to the small ring from the middle ring when the rear mech is on the largest sprocket. If it won't, you may need to adjust the small ring limit screw to allow the chain to fall a little further so it engages the small ring. You will also need to loosen the clamp bolt and release a small amount of slack cable so the mech can move down. Make this adjustment a small amount at a time, so that the chain does not end up falling off the inner ring.

Indexing

Adjusting STI front indexing is basically a matter of setting the cable tension so that the chain falls from the big to the middle ring when the upper button is pressed once. To do this, put the chain on the big ring, then press the upper button. The chain should drop smoothly to the middle ring. If it overshoots, unscrew the barrel adjuster on the shifter to tighten the cable. If the chain doesn't drop to the middle ring, screw the barrel adjuster in until it does. If there is insufficient adjustment possible, loosen the clamp bolt, screw the adjuster out to create some slack, then retighten the cable and adjust accordingly.

Routine maintenance

All a front derailleur really needs is to feel loved; keep it clean and lube the pivot points and cables regularly and it'll last ages. To lube the cables, put the mech on the big ring, then set the shifter to the small-ring position. This creates enough slack to allow you to pull the cables out of the slots in the stops. Wipe them with a clean rag soaked in lubricant.

6: Brakes

Broadly, there are two types of brakes in common use on mountain bikes; cantilevers, which have their braze-on pivots below the level of the rim, and U-brakes, which have pivots above the rim. Both types have their advantages, though cantilevers are by far the more common.

Cantilever brakes

The switch from heavy, indifferently functioning hub brakes to light, efficient cantilevers was one of the things which transformed the original California clunkers into proper mountain bikes. Since then cantilevers have evolved from the Mafacs that were all there was in the early eighties to sophisticated stoppers of today like Shimano's Deore XT or SunTour's XC-Pro SE units. Cantilever designs of one sort or another now rule the roost after the industry's disastrous dalliance with under-the-chainstay, in-the-mud brakes in 1988, and virtually all brakes on mountain bikes are now mounted on the seatstays.

Cleaning cantilever brakes

Spray water at 'em! Happily, cantilever brakes have no inconvenient, fragile bearings

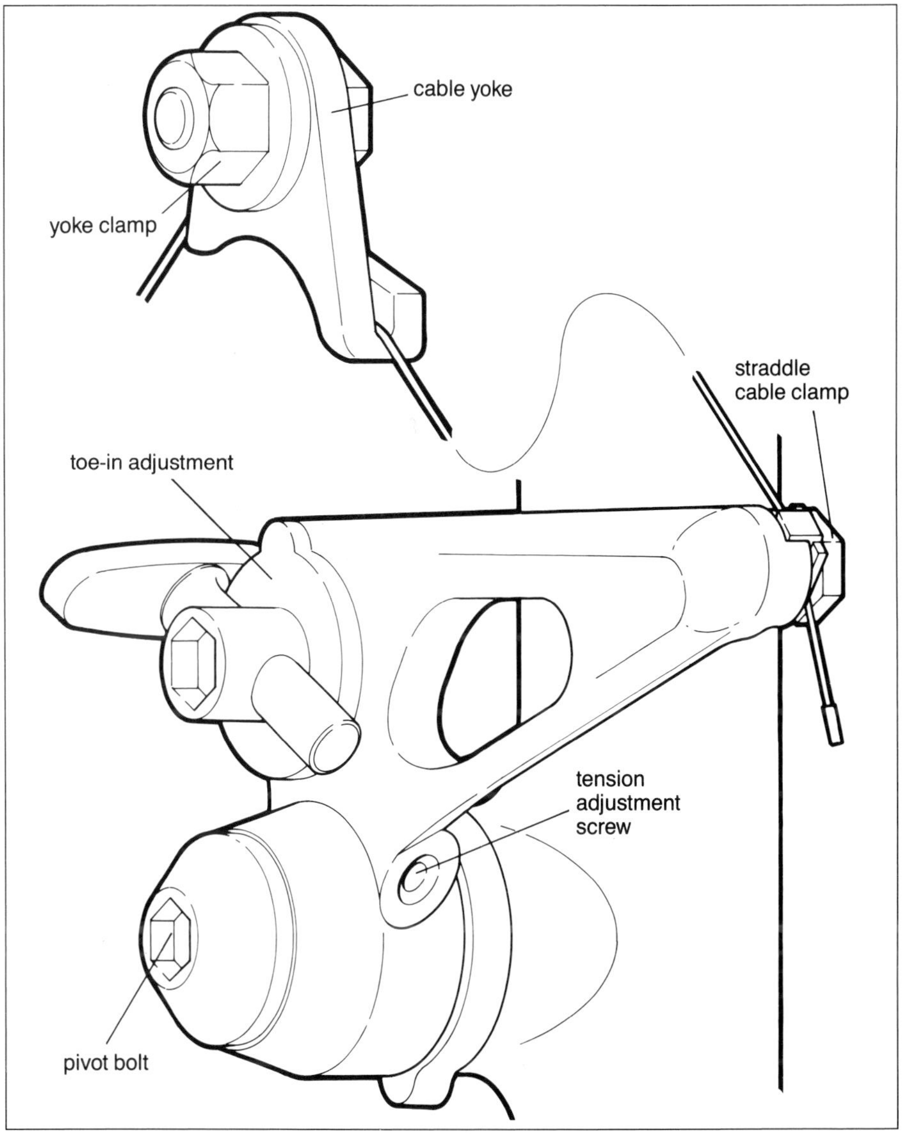

cable yoke

yoke clamp

straddle cable clamp

toe-in adjustment

tension adjustment screw

pivot bolt

Cantilever brake

that will get destroyed by the slightest ingress of moisture. Actually that's not quite true, since they do have steel springs and bronze bushes which could conceivably get seized up. When you've washed off the mud, spray the pivots with a thin penetrating lube (LPS1, Superspray Lube, Cyclon) to drive out any water that's crept in.

While you've got your can of lube in hand, spray a little on the pivot point in the lever to keep it moving freely and lube the cables. This is easy if your bike has slotted cable stops (as most now do). Unhook the straddle cable quick release (QR) to produce some slack, pull the outer away from the stop, move it along the cable and lube each bit as it is exposed until you've done the whole cable. The easiest way to lube the exposed cable is to spray some on a cloth and use that to wipe the cable. Put the outer back in the stops and reconnect the QR.

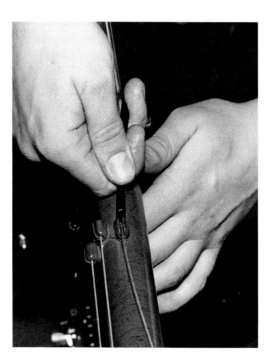

Removing outer cables from stops for lubricating

When you've got them clean, it's time to check the brake blocks for wear and tear. Most blocks have little water-dispersing grooves cut into them, and the manufacturers say you should replace them when the block has worn to the bottom of the grooves. This usually means throwing away a brake block which has half its useful pad material left, but since most brake blocks consist of pad material moulded around a metal body, it is essential to replace them before they get down to the metal, since these metal cores can seriously damage rims. This means it is better to err on the side of caution and follow the manufacturers advice.

Blocks can also damage rims if chips of rock or metal get embedded in them and score the sidewall of the rim. A chunk of rock can do irreparable damage fairly quickly, so it's worth checking the blocks for particles quite often. To do this, push them into the rim, pull out the straddle wire and allow the brake to spring open. You can now see the braking surfaces and should dig out any intruding objects with a sharp implement.

Replacing cantilever brake blocks

There are two types of cantilever brake block; bolt-type and stud-type. Time was, all cantilevers took stud-type blocks and bolt types were for side-pulls, but the introduction of Shimano's Exage components and the cheaper Dia-Compe cantilevers heralded the use of special bolt-type blocks on some cantilevers.

In short, Shimano 200GS, Deore DX and Deore XT cantilevers take stud-type blocks, all other Shimano use bolt-type on their U-brakes and stud-type on their cantilevers, and this usually means Shimano Exage blocks if you can find them. Some other bolt-type blocks also work, though they'll be fiddlier

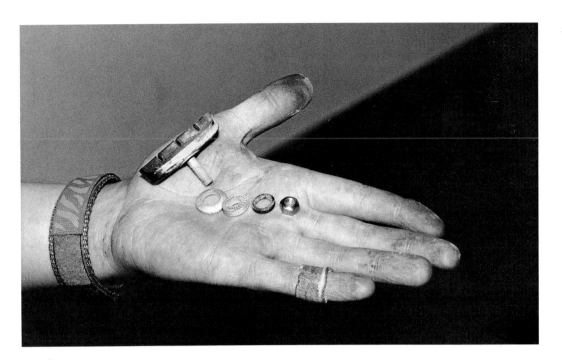

to fit. SunTour XCD, XC-Comp and XC-Pro brakes use stud-type, most other brakes fitted on SunTour-equipped bikes (actually Dia-Compe brakes for the most part) use bolt-type, though versions of Dia-Compe's low profile 986 cantilever seem to be appearing all over the place on newer bikes and these take stud-type blocks.

The advantage of stud-type blocks is that you can replace them with any other stud-type block. This means that you can put Aztecs, Kool-Stops or Mathauser blocks in place of the original, frankly, usually indifferent ones. As an aside to this I still find it odd that the Big S fits Aztec blocks to its U-brakes, but puts its own blocks on cantilevers.

All three of these aftermarket blocks work better than any of the standard blocks from Shimano, SunTour or Dia-Compe, and are the easiest and cheapest way of upgrading your brakes.

Fitting new brake blocks

Before you fit any new blocks, first screw the barrel adjusters on the levers and cable stops right in. This should release enough slack in the cable so the new blocks will fit.

To fit stud-type blocks, open the brake's quick release, remove the old ones by undoing the nut and bolt which holds them and slip the new ones into their place. To prevent the brakes from squealing the blocks should then be adjusted so that they are slightly 'toed-in', that is, the front of the block hits the rim just before the back. Pre-'91 Shimano brakes have an angle adjuster which adjusts the toe-in, most others use a curved surface on the caliper body and curved washers, which works, but doesn't always hold the blocks quite as firmly.

Shimano's angle adjust washer is very handy, but takes a bit of trial and error to learn exactly how to use it, since rotating it one way will affect each brake differently.

To tighten a stud-type block, hold it in place by hand and tighten the nut until it will hold the block. Then clamp it down firmly by holding the front of the clamp with an Allen key and tightening the nut with the appropriate spanner.

To fit bolt-type blocks, open the quick release, undo the old blocks and take them out. Put the new ones in their place. Bolt-type blocks usually have a system of curved washers to adjust the toe-in, and again the way to learn to use these is by trial and error; tighten the block gently, so it will still move but doesn't slip down in the brake, then tweak it into position and tighten it firmly. Sometimes a small adjustable spanner on the block itself is useful to stop it rotating as the nut is tightened.

Brake cables

If screwing in the barrel adjusters hasn't freed-up enough cable to allow the brake to be reconnected, then let out a small amount of the straddle wire or brake cable. The straddle wire is the easiest option; undo the cable clamp bolt and let enough of the cable through so that the QR will close.

Cables should be replaced if they are showing any significant signs of wear or fraying. If in doubt, replace them.

There have been a few nasty accidents recently when front brake cables have broken, allowing the straddle wire to fall on to the front tyre and stop the bike abruptly, catapulting the rider over the bars. Leaving a fork-mounted front reflector in place will prevent this, as will regular cable maintenance.

Switching to beefy 2mm cables like Clark's, Shimano or Odyssey will improve braking power and feel, though they do need their own wide outers which may not fit the stops and levers on some bikes.

To replace a frayed, worn or damaged cable, undo the cable clamp bolt at the straddle yoke and pull the old cable out of the yoke, outers and levers. If you're replacing the outers, hang on to the old ones so you can use them as a guide to cut the new ones to length.

Cut the outer to length, aiming to run it in smooth curves with no sharp turns. Use proper cable cutters rather than pliers (SunTour and Shimano both do good ones). File the ends of the outer smooth to remove any burrs the cable could snag on. Fill the outers with lube, using the little tube that comes with the can.

Thread the new cable into the brake lever, through the outers and stops and through the yoke. Hold the brake pads on to the rim with a third-hand tool or toestrap and tighten the yoke bolt firmly.

Brake levers

Most brake levers have an alloy body which clamps the bar and is tightened with an Allen key. Pre-STI Shimano Exage levers have a cross-head screw inside the lever body. Brake levers need to be tight, but not so tight that they break rather than move in a crash.

Virtually all levers have some sort of adjustment for the distance from the lever to the bar. XT and DX levers have a four-position adjuster under the lever, all others have a screw on the inboard side of the body, which needs either a screwdriver or the appropriate Allen key. The lever position affects the cable adjustment, so set it first, before changing the blocks or cables.

A cable puller and third hand tool make brake adjustment easier

Tighten the cable yoke clamp firmly – you don't want the cable to pull through at an inopportune moment

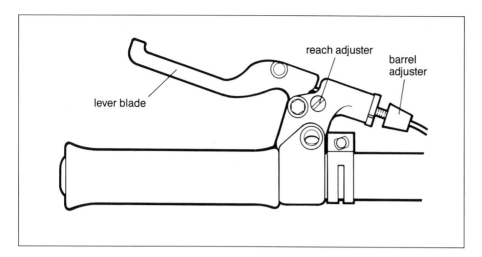

lever blade
reach adjuster
barrel adjuster

Brake lever

Post-1991 Shimano cantilevers

Since 1991 almost all Shimano cantilevers use a link wire and cable carrier which join the brake cable directly to one cantilever arm. To set these up you need a set of Shimano cable setting tools, colour-coded and marked with a number which is also found on the appropriate link wire.

Using the plastic Shimano guide to adjust the cantilevers

Brake levers can usually be reach-adjusted by some means or other. These Shimano levers have a screw slot on their underside. Other models may use grub screws on their inside edge

To correctly set up a post-1991 Shimano cantilever, run the brake cable through the cable carrier, tighten the cable clamp bolt enough that it holds the cable but it will still pull through, and fit the setting tool into place under the link wire and cable.

Pull the cable through, and check that the carrier is centred and the ends of the brake setting tool touch the cantilever arms. Tighten the cable clamp bolt on the cantilever, then the one on the cable carrier.

To adjust the brake pads, leave the setting tool in place and loosen the brake pad clamps. Move the pads in so that they touch the rim, using the lines on the brake pad studs to set them evenly, then tighten the clamps with the pads touching the rims. Removing the brake setting tool will create the correct space between the rim and blocks.

Adjusting cantilever brakes

All that remains is to make sure that the blocks are a sensible, equal distance from the rim. There should be a 2mm gap between the rim and block on each side, and the blocks shouldn't rub the rim when you spin the wheel.

The easiest way to adjust the total amount of gap is to change the straddle wire length. Loosen the straddle wire clamp bolt and pull the cable through with a cable tensioner (fourth-hand tool) or pliers, then tighten the clamp up firmly. (It's important that both the straddle wire clamp and yoke clamp are very tight; the last thing you want is for your cables to pull through at a critical moment!)

Shimano brakes have a 2mm Allen key screw buried in the right hand side of the caliper which is used to even up the brake

SunTour brakes need cone spanners to adjust the tension

Centring a Shimano cantilever with a 2mm Allen key

Always grease cantilever pivots before installation to avoid the brakes binding

tension, providing you can find your 2mm Allen key; mine always seems to find the most obscure corner of the toolbox to hide in!

Troubleshooting

The most common fault with brakes is sticky or worn cables; keep them well-lubed and replace them as we've detailed above and they shouldn't give you any hassle. If the brake calipers don't spring back properly even though the cables are lubricated they may be sticking on the pivot. To check for this unbolt the caliper from the frame and check that there is no paint on the pivot. Sand it off with fine emery cloth if there is and smear grease on it afterwards.

U-brakes

There was a time when it was practically impossible to buy a production mountain bike that didn't have the rear brake tucked away under the bottom bracket. Cantilevers dominated the early mountain bike brake scene, just as they do now, but for eighteen months or so from the end of '87 to early '89, brakes changed shape and ran and hid under the chainstays where, we were confidently told by manufacturers, they were going to stay for ever more because they were better there. Wrong!

It quickly transpired that under the bottom bracket was the worst possible place for a brake in the wet, muddy conditions that prevailed in the 'summer' of '88. U-brakes were blamed for jamming the chain, causing the bike to clog with mud, slowing the removal of the rear wheel, filing tyre sidewalls, and not working any better than cantilevers, so why bother?   .

History

Well, the U-brake originally appeared as part of Shimano's ongoing struggle with SunTour for domination of the world mountain bike components market. Back in the pre-SIS mid-eighties SunTour looked to have the edge. Their gears worked better than Shimano's and their ultra-powerful Power-cam rear brake was the choice of most American mountain bike pros. SIS was one prong of Shimano's attack on SunTour's technical superiority and the U-brake, a scaled up version of the centre-pull brakes that were once popular on touring bikes, was the other.

SIS, of course, was a great success, and the rest is history, but the U-brake bombed. It was only a bit more powerful than the company's best cantilevers, weighed a lot more, and its position under the chainstays gave rise to a bunch of other problems. The Power-cam it was intended to compete with was a lot more powerful than a cantilever, and therefore needed the support of a large, stiff chainstay. The U-brake was positioned under the stays to give the same lines as a Power-cam, but it was sufficiently less powerful that burying it under the stays was totally unnecessary. Many riders soon realised that they'd be better off with rear cantilevers, had their frames modified accordingly and the swing back to cantilevers began. Nowadays, getting a hardcore rider to use a U-brake would be like getting a chronic spider-hater to sit still for all of *Arachnophobia*.

This is a pity, because U-brakes do still have some significant uses. Mounted on the seatstays, where rim brakes belong, they work excellently and are especially suitable for smaller riders who would catch their heels on cantilevers. Shimano made this possible by producing a booster plate to tie the pivots together and one or two small US companies make a similar device to fit U-brakes from companies like Dia-Compe. Small riders in search of bikes that fit properly should not narrow down their scope by dismissing U-brake equipped bikes as long as the brake is on the seatstays.

Maintenance of U-brakes

Shimano dominate the U-brake market now. Dia-Compe did produce a version of the idea, but since Dia-Compe brakes tend to appear on SunTour equipped bikes, and SunTour have made narrow-profile cantilevers for some time, Dia-Compe U-brakes are rare, and SunTour's Power-cam brake was really too expensive to make a big impact on production bikes.

Refer to the *Cantilever brakes* section above for details of lever and cable maintenance; this is the same for both types of brake.

Both Dia-Compe and Shimano brakes are pretty well sealed and will therefore stand hosing, though care should be taken not to drive water into the bottom bracket if you are dealing with an under-chainstay brake. A little thin lube (Cyclon, Super spray Lube, WD-40) should be used around the pivots to displace any remaining water.

One occasional problem with U-brakes is that mud can accumulate between the arms of the brake, and on the blocks. If mud in these areas has dried on to the point where it won't wash off, scrape it out with a screwdriver. Hard, dried mud on the blocks of U-brakes seems to be a cause of worn tyre sidewalls, so it is important to keep them clean.

U-brake block replacement

All Shimano U-brakes use bolt-type blocks. Shimano's own blocks are practically essential as replacements for Exage brakes, which require very deep blocks but good aftermarket units like Aztecs and Kool-stops will fit to Deore brakes. Shimano U-brakes have no toe-in facility built into the brake, so it is necessary to get blocks which have curved washers to allow you to toe them in.

The old blocks will undo with a 10mm spanner; replace them when the water-dispersing grooves are worn out, or shortly thereafter. Undo the brake's quick release first, so that fitting the blocks will not be impeded by the cable, which will probably be shorter than necessary, and screw the barrel adjuster on the brake lever all the way in.

Slip the new blocks into the slots in the brake arms, position them approximately correctly and gently tighten the nuts to hold them loosely in place. Try to re-connect the straddle wire at this point, and if it won't reach, loosen the cable clamp bolt on the yoke and let enough cable through that the straddle will reach. Tighten the yoke cable clamp bolt very firmly.

The easy way to adjust the toe-in on Shimano and Aztec blocks is to put a couple of pieces of thin card under the rear edge of the block and set the block up so the card is held in place when the lever is pulled and the front edge of the block touches the rim. With practice you can gauge this amount of toe-in by eye, though holding the block in place can be awkward.

The block should be positioned as low as possible on the rim, because U-brake blocks tend to move up the rim as they wear, and can end up filing the sidewalls of the tyre,

resulting in an expensive and dangerous blow-out. Check the block position every time you take up the cable slack.

Dia-Compe U-brakes tend to have stud-type blocks, held in a mounting bolt which has a 5mm Allen key in the front and a 10mm nut at the back. Toe-in on these brakes is adjusted by sliding the entire block and mounting around on the curved surface of the brake arm, then tightening the nut when the block is in the correct position.

Spacing

All Shimano U-brakes use a 2mm Allen key in the left-hand side brake arm to adjust the spring tension and therefore the spacing of the blocks. Dia-Compe brakes use a large nut behind the mounting bolt, which can be turned with a spanner if the mounting bolt is loosened slightly.

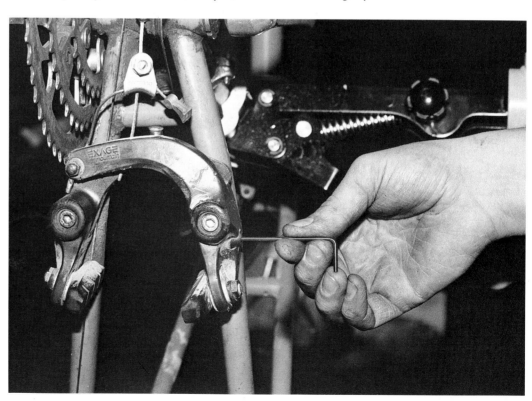

Centring a U-brake using a 2mm Allen key

Fitting

One advantage of U-brakes is that they are extremely reliable and easy to fit. This means that in practice they don't often go wrong, and the most common reason for replacing a U-brake is simply to upgrade it to a better model.

Because the spring system of U-brakes is totally self-enclosed, there is no need to fit the spring into a hole in the boss. In fact all you do to fit a new U-brake is grease the pivots, slip the brake arms onto them, grease the clamp bolt threads, screw them in loosely, hold the blocks as far apart as they will go to tension the springs and tighten the clamp bolts. Then adjust the spring tension as above. For Dia-Compe brakes, hold the spring tension adjusters as you tighten the clamp bolts.

The straddle wire is exactly the same as a cantilever straddle wire, and is best run as short as possible to increase brake power. Bear in mind that GT bikes and clones thereof need the straddle wire to cross over around the plastic cable guide on the seat tube, otherwise the rear brake will not work properly.

Hints and tips

If you still have a frame with a U-brake under the bottom bracket it is possible to have a framebuilder move it to the seatstays or fit cantilever bosses. Bear in mind that you will need to get cable stops fitted on the top tube, a bridge at the top of the seatstays and a respray or at least touch-up job on the paint.

The easiest way to get a rear wheel out of a bike which has an under chainstay U-brake is to open the wheel quick release, pull the wheel out of the drop-out and push the wheel into the brake. This will cause the

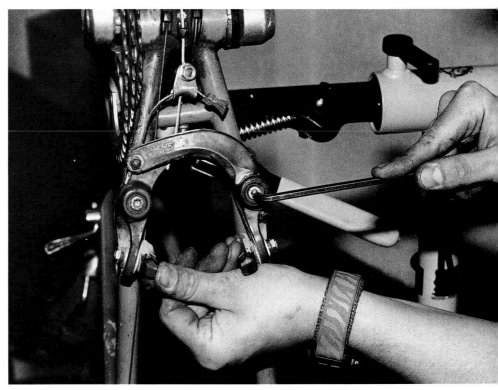

Tensioning a U-brake

ends of the brake arms to come together and the straddle wire will drop out of the hook arm.

Finally, when replacing a wheel in a frame which has both horizontal drop-outs and an under-chainstay brake, take care to position the wheel correctly in the drop-outs. Pulling the wheel too far back will allow the blocks to abrade the tyre sidewalls.

7: Chainset and bottom bracket

Your feet rest on pedals, the pedals are attached to cranks and hiding between your feet is the bearing the cranks run on, the curiously-named bottom bracket. The complete set of cranks, chainrings and bottom bracket is called a chainset, and it all turns on the bottom bracket bearing.

The bottom bracket

All your pedalling effort goes through the bottom bracket and there is a school of thought that considers it to be the most important bearing on the bike. Certainly it's one of the most annoying if anything goes wrong with it, since a loose bottom bracket is one of the main sources of mysterious clicking and creaking noises during pedalling.

Broadly there are two types of bottom bracket. By far the most common is the standard cup and cone type. This has two bearing cups which screw into each side of the frame and an axle with curved, conical bearing surfaces which the cranks bolt onto. The bearings run between the cup and cone, and almost all bike bearings are functionally identical to this, though the details differ.

'Sealed' or, more correctly, 'cartridge bearing' bottom brackets use one-piece cartridge bearings which incorporate balls and bearing surfaces in a ring-shaped unit that also includes neoprene or steel seals and is difficult or impossible to dismantle and service. These bearing units are press-fitted either into cups which screw into the frame, or directly into the frame, and slide onto the axle. There are several types, from the easily dismantled sets used by Gary Fisher, where the bearings are held in the frame with circlips and the axle is retained with grub-screw lockrings to the inexpensive use-it-for-a-year-and-throw-it-away plastic-bodied FAG bottom bracket. Most sealed bearing bottom brackets are not suitable for home servicing.

Both sealed and cup-and-cone bottom brackets come in two variants, nut-type, where the cranks are held onto the axle with a nut, and bolt-type, where the cranks are fixed by, surprise, surprise, a bolt. Cranks are generally more prone to coming loose from nut-type bottom brackets, for reasons that are somewhat esoteric, so if you are faced with a choice of a replacement axles, go for a bolt-type part.

Whatever type of bottom bracket you have, the symptoms of wear and maladjustment are much the same: 'graunching' or clicking noises from the cranks while pedalling, and cranks that can be rocked slightly from side to side (at right angles to their normal direction of rotation) are usually indications of a loose or worn bottom bracket.

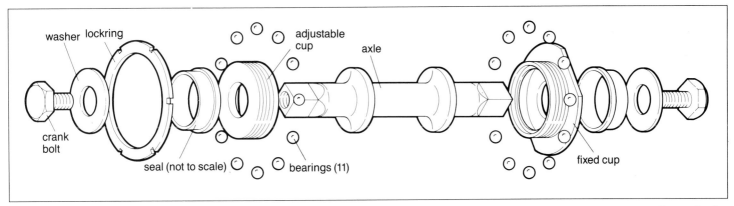

If the cranks will not turn freely, then the bottom bracket is too tight. To check for this, drop the chain off the inside of the chainrings and spin the cranks. It'll be readily apparent if the bottom bracket is stiff; the cranks won't spin freely, but instead they'll slow down after a couple of revolutions or less. If you've any of these symptoms in a FAG, Tioga or SunTour cartridge bearing bottom bracket, then it'll need replacing. The FAG needs a special tool which should be available from any shop that stocks the bottom bracket. The Tioga is removed with standard bottom bracket tools, but the SunTour also needs special tools; again consult a bike shop. These three units are almost unknown on production bikes.

If the bottom bracket is not loose or over-tight, then a clicking noise may be due to a slightly loose crank, and this should be tightened up as explained below.

Unlike many parts of a bike which can be repaired with just screwdrivers, spanners and Allen keys, bottom brackets do require special tools to dismantle and reassemble them properly. The minimum you'll need is a crank extractor, a lockring spanner and an adjustable cup spanner (also known as a peg spanner.) Madison do inexpensive versions of

these tools, including adjustable ones for odd-sized cups and lockrings. A set of these is relatively cheap at the other end of the scale are Campag, Shimano or Park tools – these will set you back a great deal more, but are pro quality and last forever; worth considering for a club workshop. They also fit SunTour and Sugino bottom brackets. Somewhere in between in price are Tacx tools, which are good personal workshop units.

Probably the most important thing to remember about good, specialist bike tools like these is **never lend them to anyone**. By all means let people use them, but good bike tools have a habit of never being seen again if you loan them out, which is what happened to the last set of Tacx bottom bracket tools I had. If you're out there somewhere, Phil Robinson, I'd like my spanners back please!

Removing the cranks

The first thing you'll need to do to service an errant bottom bracket is remove the cranks to get at the bottom bracket cups. First take the dust caps off the end of the crank. Some, like Shimano Exage and SunTour XCE dust

Removing crank dustcaps with needle-nosed pliers

the original Allen key hole a screwdriver blade the right size can sometimes be forced in to turn the cap. Alternatives include cutting a slot in the cap with a saw, if it has enough of a raised portion above the crank, (avoid cutting the crank!), drilling holes in the cap and turning it with needle nosed pliers and drilling down the thread to break the cap. As a last resort plastic dustcaps can be burnt out with a brazing torch. All of these are pro mechanics' desperate measures and should not be attempted by novices who might easily do more damage than good.

Behind the dustcap is a 14mm nut or bolt and washer. The crank extractor has a socket to match in the unthreaded end, so use this to remove the nut or bolt. Campagnolo and TA bolts are both 15mm and need the special 15mm socket spanner these companies make to remove them. (An ordinary socket spanner will almost certainly be too large to fit in the hole in the crank.) All others are 14mm. Remember to take the washer out as well as the bolt.

Next screw the crank extractor into the thread in the crank arm. It should fit snugly, without rattling in the thread, but should go in without needing undue pressure from a spanner. If the extractor is tight or loose in the threads or is not in absolutely straight, it can damage the threads and should not be used. If in doubt consult your local bike dealer. Problems of this type are less likely if you use the same brand of extractor as your cranks, and keep the crank threads clean.

With the extractor fitted in the crank it can now be used to pull the crank off the axle. Turn the inner part of the extractor clockwise with a spanner until the crank falls off the axle. Repeat the procedure for the other crank.

caps, just pop out of the threads while others need a 5-mm Allen key and still others have a slot and can be removed with a coin. Shimano Deore dustcaps have two little holes in them and can be removed with needle nosed pliers or half a spoke, bent over so the ends fit in the holes. Dust caps are important for keeping the extractor threads in the crank arm clean; don't throw them away.

It's not unknown for dustcaps to seize in the crank threads, and if this happens there are a number of ways of liberating them, though the more extreme methods require specialist tools, like a brazing torch. What usually happens is that the first attempt to remove the cap wrecks the Allen key hole or slot, leaving you standing there feeling foolish, and wondering what the hell to do next. The first avenue is always to drench the whole area in Duckoil or WD-40, leave it for a few hours to work its way into the thread, then try to shift the cap. If there's anything left of

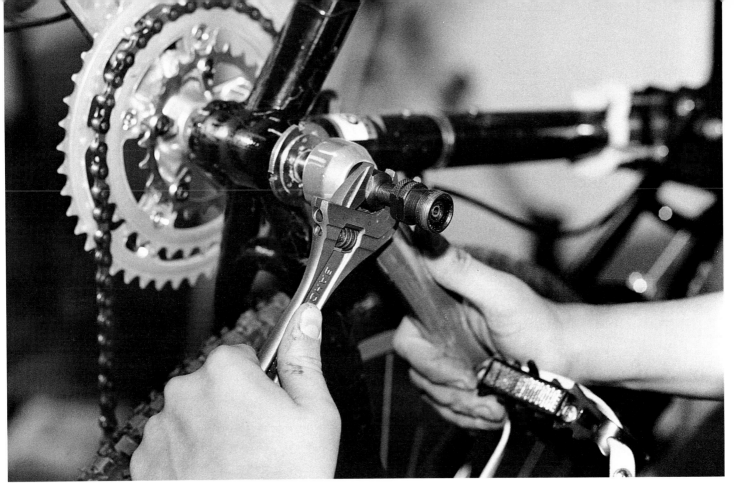

Loosening the crank retaining bolt

Pushing the crank off the axle with a
crank extractor. Ensure that the extractor
is screwed right into the crank arm

Stripped threads

If the extractor threads are damaged, or the end of the crank has become damaged, preventing the extractor from going in, you'll need to resort to rather more extreme methods of getting the crank off. VAR make a special tool which grabs the crank and pushes against the axle to get it off, but like most methods of removing damaged cranks it tends to write them off, by bending them. If you're going to tackle removing a stripped crank, be prepared to replace it afterwards.

The simplest method of getting a stripped crank off is to take the bolt out and hit the back of the crank with a hammer, using a twelve-inch-long piece of half-inch steel bar (a drift), just next to the axle. Eventually the crank will fly across the room. Make sure there's no-one in the way!

A subtler technique is to use an automotive gear puller, which has two arms to grip the

back of the crank and a 'pusher' which pushes against the axle. This can be difficult to use on right hand cranks, since it is awkward to get the arms evenly spaced; the five arm spider gets in the way.

With both of these techniques there is a chance of getting the crank off intact, though I wouldn't want to have a stripped crank lying around the place, even as a spare – someone might try to use it. The last method destroys the square taper, but has the advantage of needing no special tools, Just take off the crank bolt and continue to ride the bike. Sooner or later the crank will work loose and drop off. Make sure you have a spare to hand when it does!

You'll now have a bare bottom bracket. Remove the adjustable cup by loosening off the lockring and unscrewing the cup from the frame with the peg spanner. Pull out the axle and fixed cup bearings and sleeve, if

Undoing the bottom bracket lockring

there is one. The fixed has left-hand thread and therefore unscrews clockwise, unless you have an Italian bike which has right-hand threads on both sides. It can be cleaned in situ with a rag and solvent but will need removing if you want to check it for wear. Clean the cups, axle and bearings with solvent. Examine the bearing surfaces and balls for signs of wear. A smooth track where the balls run on the cup is OK, but if there are craters or pits in these tracks then the damaged component should be replaced, as should the balls which will no longer be perfectly spherical.

Replacing the bottom bracket

When obtaining replacement parts from a dealer, take the old ones with you. It's much easier for shop workers to find a replacement part if they've got the original to work from, than to deduce what it is from a vague description. The only parts that are the same for almost all bottom brackets are the ball bearings which are quarter-inch in size and twenty-two in number (eleven per side.) Make sure you get proper industrial quality bearings such as RHP or FAG, not 'steel balls' which are about as round as cake decorations, but not as tasty.

In general it's better to replace caged balls with loose ones, as the replacement cages available usually come with low quality bearings. Loose balls are easier to service and clean and you can get more balls in, spreading the load and prolonging the life of all the components of the bottom bracket. In theory caged balls reduce ball to ball friction, but in practice this is a minor consideration. Getting dirty grease out of a caged bearing is so much hassle that it's just not worth it.

The disassembled parts of a bottom bracket, consisting of a lockring, adjustable cup, caged bearing, axle, sleeve and fixed cup

Before re-installing the bottom bracket, clean out the inside of the bottom bracket shell in the frame with solvent and a rag, to prevent the newly cleaned pieces from picking up dirt and grit. Smear clean grease on the inside of the cups and place the balls in it, eleven per cup. Put more grease over the top of the balls to stick them in place. Grease the fixed cup and fit it in the right hand (transmission) side of the bottom bracket shell, remembering to screw it in anti-clockwise, if it's left-hand threaded. It should be possible to fit it initially by hand or with only very light force from a spanner. If it is very stiff it may be cross-threaded or the threads may need a clearing tap running through them, a job for a bike shop. If you screw a cross-threaded cup into a frame you may do very expensive damage, so proceed cautiously. Fixed cups need to be in as tight as possible to prevent them from coming loose under pedalling loads.

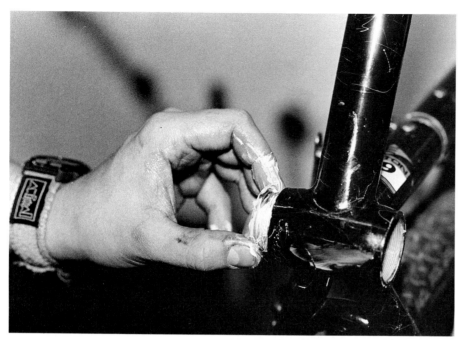

Grease the fixed cup and screw it back with the bearings in place

The sleeve goes in next, followed by the axle. Most mountain bike axles are asymmetrical, having a longer end on the drive side. Take care not to dislodge any of the balls from the fixed cup when fitting the axle.

Grease the adjustable cup thread next and screw it into the frame until it stops against the axle. Fit the lockring onto the cup and adjust the cup so that the axle turns smoothly with no play. Tighten the lockring while holding the cup in place with the peg spanner. Check the axle for play. Usually, tightening the lockring produces a small amount of play in the bottom bracket because it pushes on the frame and pulls out the cup. If this has happened, loosen the lockring and adjust the cup so that the bearing is slightly stiff. You may need to

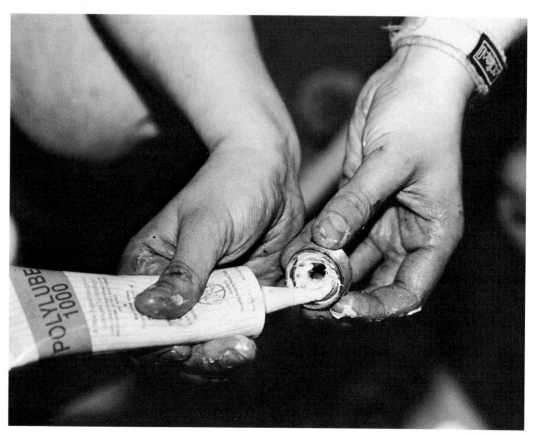

Pack the adjustable cup bearings with grease

repeat this procedure a couple of times to get it spot on.

If you are at all unsure of how to carry on, at any stage in the reassembling of a bottom bracket, ask your local bike specialist. We once had a very irate customer return to the shop with a wrecked bottom bracket: he'd forced the cups into the wrong sides of the frame, and just for good measure, screwed the pedals into the wrong cranks. All new equipment, all expensively ruined, and it was, he claimed, all our fault because we hadn't told him how to fit them. Since he hadn't asked, we'd assumed he knew what he was doing – if you interrogated everyone who buys anything on a busy Saturday about their mechanical knowledge you'd go bust! If in doubt, ask.

Replacing the cranks

First clean any excess grease off the ends of the axle, and clean the inside of the crank arms. Greasy cranks can slide too far on to the axle, weakening the crank. Slide the cranks on to the axle, fit the nuts or bolts and washers and tighten them with the socket end of the crank extractor. Remember to put the cranks at one hundred and eighty degrees to each other. (You may well laugh, but I've seen some experienced mechanics leap cheerfully onto hastily assembled bikes, only to find the cranks at ninety degrees!) Crank bolts should be tightened up hard – limit of strength with an eight inch spanner is about right for most people.

If you've got threaded dustcaps, grease them. A seized steel dustcap is a first class hassle to remove. For this reason I prefer plastic dustcaps – they're lighter, self lubricating and can be melted out if necessary.

Screw in the adjustable cup with a peg spanner. It might take several attempts to get the bearings adjusted properly

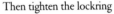

Then tighten the lockring

Replacing the chainrings

Chainrings wear out. It's not surprising really: they're usually made from aluminium alloy, whilst chains are made from hardened steel. The usual symptom of a worn chainring is the chain slipping in all the gears, but only on one chainring, and it's usually the middle ring that goes first, since it gets the most use. The solution is to replace the ring.

Outer and middle chainrings are relatively easy to remove with the crank on the bike, but to get at the inner ring you'll need to take off the right-hand crank, as described above. The rings are held on with 5-mm Allen key bolts of a design which is unique to chainsets. The inner ring has five bolts which screw directly into the inside of the crank arms and the middle and outer rings

are linked by nut-and-bolt pairs that go through the ends of the crank spider arms. Unscrew all the necessary bolts and put them somewhere safe, along with any spacers or nuts that come with them.

The outer ring is usually big enough to pass comfortably over the pedal, and the middle ring will usually fit over with a bit of fiddling, but if you've got large pedals you may need to take the pedal off. To do this you need a 15mm pedal spanner. Unscrew the pedal anti-clockwise. (See **Chapter 11** for more on pedals.)

There is a wide variety of replacement chainrings available and the main differences between them are in the quality of the materials used to make them. The first difference is between aluminium alloy and stainless steel. Aluminium has been the

Removing the retaining bolts for the outer and middle chainrings. Mind your knuckles on the chainrings – they hurt!

You don't have to take the pedals off to get to the chainrings

material of choice for chainrings for years, because it is light, but there are several different grades of the material which are suitable for rings. It is worth spending the extra money on rings that are made from the harder grades of aluminium, such as Mavic, Campagnolo, SR and Shimano Deore XT rings. Very small chainrings on mountain bikes tend to wear out rapidly if they are made from aluminium, so several manufacturers have introduced steel inner rings in the last couple of years. Onza Buzz Saws and SR Ninja are the best known, but Shimano also make steel inner rings.

Replacing Shimano chainrings is complicated by the fact that their oval Biopace and Superglide chainrings are not supposed to be compatible with other brands of ring. In practice you can mix Biopace and round rings quite freely, and the same is true of Superglide and standard rings, though the front gear shifting will not be quite as quick if you substitute a normal ring for a Superglide ring. When replacing Shimano rings use Deore XT replacements that are otherwise the same as the original component.

The tab on Shimano chainrings should align with the crank arm to ensure that the Superglide works properly

Both Superglide and Biopace rings have a tab on one sector of the ring which is intended to go behind the crank arm. This tab ensures that these rings are correctly aligned, Biopace to provide its claimed biomechanical advantages and Superglide rings to give the ultra smooth shifting they are renowned for.

8: Hubs and freewheels

Hubs

Hubs perch in the middle of the wheel, like a couple of alloy spiders in a stainless steel web, usually forgotten until something goes wrong with them. This isn't often if you keep them clean and well-maintained, but will be if you tend to ride through rivers and neglect them.

Like bottom brackets, hubs come in two variants, lip-sealed cup-and-cone (standard) bearing type and 'sealed' cartridge bearing. The latter have fallen out of favour in recent years and it is still unusual to find them as original equipment on a production bike. To improve standard bearing hubs,

in 1988 Shimano introduced the freehub, a system where the freewheel was actually part of the hub, rather than a separate unit which screwed onto it. This allowed them to space the rear hub bearings further apart, strengthening the rear axle.

The SunTour/WTB Greaseguard system on the top-line XC-Pro group looked as though it might make cartridge bearing hubs popular again, but the very late availability of these components in 1990 meant that this didn't happen and probably won't for some time to come, though there are now a lot more SunTour equipped bikes out there.

Front hub

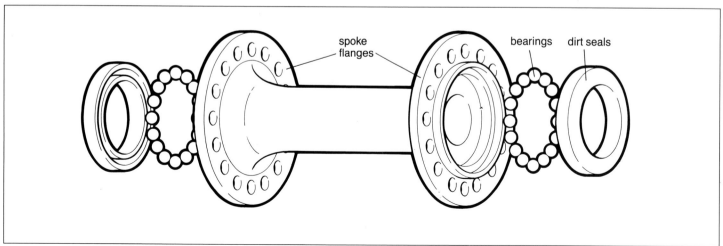

spoke flanges · bearings · dirt seals

Signs of wear and maladjustment are similar to other bearings. If the hubs are too tight or worn the axle will not turn smoothly in the hub; if they are too loose the wheel will rattle slightly in the frame. Grab the tyre and try and move it from side to side. If it moves at all, attention is needed. An over-tight hub may not be obvious while the wheel is still in the frame, so it's worth taking the wheels out occasionally to check the bearings.

A set of thin cone spanners is one of the best investments you can make. Campagnolo are the best and still quite reasonably priced. You'll need a set that consists of a pair of 13mm/14mm double ended cone spanners, a pair of 15mm/16mm units and standard 15mm, 16mm or 17mm spanners to fit the lock-nuts. The last three vary from hub to hub so take your bike with you when buying tools or use a good quality adjustable spanner.

Dismantling the front hubs

This is the easy bit! Take the wheel out of the frame and remove the axle nuts or quick release skewers and put them somewhere safe. Slip a cone spanner on one cone and a standard spanner on the adjacent lock-nut and unscrew the lock-nut anti-clockwise. Remove the lock-nut from the axle. Slide off the tab washer (if there is one) and unscrew the cone. If the cone is a tight fit it may be necessary to hold the lock-nut on the other end of the axle with a spanner while you unscrew it, but cones can usually be unscrewed by hand.

Pull the axle and remaining cones out of the hub, pop the seals out of the hub shell and tip the bearings into a plastic tub. Front hub bearings are usually 3/16 inch in size and eighteen in number, nine per side, but take one of the old ones along when buying

Loosening the front hub locknuts with thin cone spanners

replacements. It's sensible to buy a few more than this because they do tend to run away across the workshop floor and hide under large, heavy objects. With the hub shell bare you can now clean the bearing surfaces of the cup and cone and inspect them for wear. A smoothly worn bearing track is acceptable, but any sign of pitting indicates that they should be replaced. Replacement cones can be obtained from your bike shop, but replacement cup bearing surfaces are only available for Campag hubs and this is why it is vitally important to maintain them. Since most hubs, and especially Shimano freehubs, are only available as pairs, a single worn cup can land you with a hefty bill for replacement hubs and wheel-building.

Removing a front axle

Prising out the dust seals. Be ready to catch the bearings before they run all over the floor

The last thing to check is that the axle is straight. This can be done by sighting down it or rolling it along a glass sheet. If it veers to one side, it's bent and should be replaced. Take any parts you need to replace along to the shop with you.

Reassembling the front hubs

Clean the components with solvent and allow them to dry. Smear grease on the bearing cups, put the bearings in and add extra grease over the top of them. Replace the seals in the hub shell. Tighten the lock-nut and cone which remain on the axle against each other, by holding the cone and turning the lock-nut clockwise onto it. If you took off the cone to replace it, screw it back on, followed by the tab washer and lock-nut. Position the lock-nut to leave enough space on the end of the axle for it to fit in the frame. This is about 4mm for quick release hubs, 15mm-20mm for solid axle hubs.

Fit the axle into the hub, taking care not to dislodge the bearings and screw on the cone, washer and lock-nut. Screw the cone down to the bearings and set it so that the axle turns freely without play. Tighten the lock-nut down against the washer and cone, holding the cone with the cone spanner. It may take a few goes to get the adjustment exactly right, but it's worth taking the time to get them spot on. When the cones are adjusted correctly tighten them up firmly to stop them coming loose.

The rear hubs

Servicing rear hubs is complicated by the presence of a freewheel or freehub body. A conventional screw-on freewheel must be removed before the cones can be adjusted. This is done with a freewheel remover, a tool which fits in or on to the the centre of the freewheel, and turns just the inner body without involving the freewheel mechanism. (If you tried to unscrew a freewheel by turning the sprockets it would just free-wheel.)

Different freewheels need different tools to remove them, so again, take your bike along

Pack grease into the bearings. You can't put too much in

to the shop with you. The most common type are probably the Shimano Uniglide and Hyperglide, which take a splined remover, and SunTour's Accushift freewheel which takes a four-pronged tool. Do not attempt to remove a SunTour four-pronged freewheel with a two-pronged tool – this fits the old Perfect and New Winner models – because either the tool or the prongs on the freewheel may break, making it next to impossible to remove. I use a Cyclo tool which has both Shimano and SunTour fittings, and an ingenious fitting system involving a threaded tube which screws in to the axle to hold the remover in place.

As an aside to all this, if you are cutting the spokes to take the rim off a wheel in order to have it rebuilt, remove the freewheel first. A hub and freewheel are all but impossible to

separate once the wheel has been cut apart.

To remove the freewheel, place the tool in the freewheel body and hold it in place with the quick release skewer or nut. For the Cyclo tool, fit the correct end into the freewheel, screw the threaded tube on to the axle and fit the locking collar over the tube. Tighten the grub screw on the locking collar.

Clamp the tool in a vice and twist the whole wheel anti-clockwise until it starts to turn. With the freewheel thus loosened you can now remove the wheel from the vice, loosen the quick release or axle nut and unscrew the freewheel.

If you haven't got a vice, a large adjustable spanner will usually provide enough leverage to shift the freewheel, though you may need to enlist the help of another pair of arms. Once you've got the freewheel off, servicing is the same as for a front hub. Smear grease on the freewheel thread when replacing it, to stop it seizing up.

Using a freewheel remover. Freewheels are usually on pretty tight, but remember that left hand thread!

Grease freewheel threads before replacing

The hub bearings in a Shimano freehub can be serviced without removing the freehub body. The right hand side bearing is just inside the freehub body and you can get at it by removing the axle and seals. Servicing is then the same as for front hubs.

If you've got a rattly rear hub, it is almost always the freewheel side cone that has worked loose. There's no mechanical reason for this, just the native cussedness of inanimate objects. The drive side bearing is the hardest to get at; it stands to reason, then, that it's going to be the one which needs adjusting! The practical upshot of this is that there's no point trying to adjust a loose rear hub by adjusting the easily accessible left-hand bearing only, because odds-on the right hand side will also need

tweaking. The best thing to do is to start by tightening the lock-nut on the drive side cone.

Freewheels and freehubs

These have got to be the least user-serviceable parts of a bike and my general advice is leave well alone. Regular flushing with a light spray oil such as Superspray Lube or Cyclon Course will clean out the bearings and a follow-through with a heavier oil such as Cyclon MTB will keep them turning. The place to spray lubricant is the tiny gap between the outer part of the freewheel body, which moves, and the inner part, which doesn't.

If a freewheel or freehub is still excessively

graunchy, or sticks, or freewheels in both directions, and lubrication doesn't cure the problem, then frankly it is simpler to replace it than service it. One of the MBUK Northern Wrecking Crew claims to have nightmares still about the little fiddly bits of metal and rubber which sealed 1988 Shimano Deore XT freehubs. There were about a dozen of them, though it seemed like more, and it was impossible to lay them out in sequence or remember which order to put them back in. The guts of Shimano freehub bodies are now simpler, but replacement ones can be had from Shimano, and it's so much easier to just slap a new one on that it hardly seems worth trying to dismantle and service them.

Shimano freehub bodies are removed and replaced with a 10mm Allen key which fits

Freehubs are held in place with a 10mm Allen bolt

down the inside of the hub when the axle has been removed. The thread of the retaining bolt must be kept free of grease because it has to be a very tight, clean fit in the hub shell. A removing tool exists for Dura-Ace freehubs, but it will not work on *any* mountain bike freehub; you need a 10mm Allen key.

Cheaper SunTour equipped bikes still use freewheels. Again these can be serviced, in theory, but in practice it's not worth the hassle since new ones aren't expensive. More expensive SunTour groupsets are just beginning to appear with SunTour's new freehub design, which has a steel sleeve that goes right through the hub to retain the freehub body, avoiding the use of a steel bolt in a fine aluminium thread, which SunTour feel is the main disadvantage of the Shimano system. This is removed with a 9mm Allen key.

Sprockets

Attached to the outside of the freewheel or freehub are between five and eight gear sprockets. There is usually no need to do more than keep these clean until they become so worn that one or all of them needs replacing. You usually find out that this is necessary when you've just fitted a new chain and the transmission still slips because the sprocket teeth have become slightly worn. It's rare to find that all the sprockets are worn – usually just the smaller ones, or the couple you use most will be shot.

To get the sprockets off you will need a pair of chain whips, or, for Shimano Hyperglide systems, a chain whip and a Hyperglide lockring tool (TL HG-15). Most sprockets slide onto splines on the freewheel body and are held in place by a threaded top sprocket;

Shimano Hyperglide sprockets all spline into place, and are held in place with a lockring. Because Hyperglide's incredibly fast and smooth shifts rely on precise alignment of the pickup teeth and release teeth on adjacent sprockets it is essential that they are aligned properly, and so the sprockets have one spline which is larger than the others to force correct fitting.

To remove the sprockets, first wrap a chain whip around a sprocket in the middle of the block so that it pulls the freewheel clockwise. To remove sprockets from a standard freewheel, wrap the other chain whip around the top sprocket so it pulls anti-clockwise. Position the two chain whips so that the handles cross and you can undo the top sprocket by squeezing them together with both hands. This may require a considerable amount of force, especially if the cluster has been used for a long time, which is why the mechanic I mentioned in Chapter 2 ended up with a home-made set of Armageddon chain whips for shifting stubborn top sprockets.

Hyperglide freewheels come off far more easily. After you've positioned the first chain whip, put the Hyperglide lockring tool in the lockring and attach a large adjustable spanner to it. Turn the lockring tool anti-clockwise while holding the sprockets with the chain whip.

Once you've got the top sprocket or lockring off the rest will just slide off the freewheel body. Most sprocket clusters are made up of separate sprockets that slide individually on to the body, but Hyperglide clusters are held together by long bolts that thread in from the back of the cluster, or by rivets. The bolts can be unscrewed with a 3mm spanner or pliers, but the riveted sets can't be easily dismantled and must be replaced as a

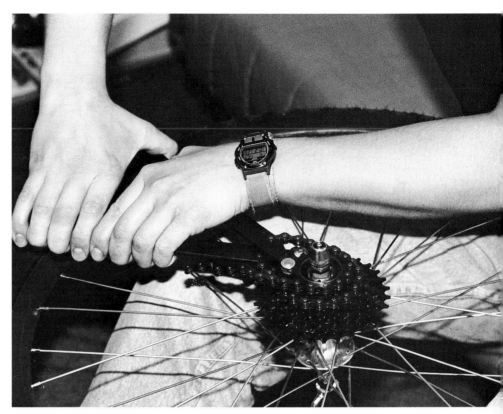

Removing sprockets with a pair of chain whips. Mind your fingers!

Removing a Hyperglide lockring

A removed freehub cluster and lockring

complete set. Take the whole lot, or just the ones that are slipping, down to the bike shop and get replacements.

To re-fit sprockets, slide the new ones and spacers back onto the freewheel body and screw the top sprocket back on. There is no need to take a chain whip to the top sprocket to tighten it up, just make sure that when you first ride the bike you do so with the chain on the top sprocket to snug it down. For Hyperglide clusters, screw in the

lockring and tighten it with the lockring tool and a large adjustable spanner. It must be tight; a loose lockring means sprockets falling off in the middle of nowhere, and you won't have a TL HG-15 with you when this happens.

Another reason why you might want to change sprockets is to change the gearing of your mountain bike. I run the standard 12-28 cluster for racing and fun riding, but switch to a 13-30 or 14-32 for touring, and

Shimano even make a 13-34 that provides ultra-low gearing for heavily laden, steep tours. You are restricted to the standard clusters Shimano offer if you want to run Hyperglide, but SunTour and non-Hyperglide Shimano systems allow you to mix and match sprockets to create custom gear systems.

How gears work

To understand gears, you need to know how to calculate a gear ratio, and the way these are quoted is a bit odd. We talk about gears in inches, but this number is not, as you might expect, the distance along the ground that one turn of the pedals would take you. To find out what it means we have to take a short trip back to the 1870s when 'Ordinary' or 'penny farthing' bikes were used. These early machines had a large front wheel which was driven directly by the pedals without chains or gears. The larger the front wheel the faster you could go for a given pedalling speed, which is why they got so big in the first place. The gear of one of these bikes was expressed in terms of the size of the wheel, and when chain driven bikes began to appear the manufacturers quoted their gear sizes in terms of the size of wheel an Ordinary would need, to have the same gear. It's archaic, but the system has survived to this day.

To work out a gear ratio, divide the number of teeth on the chainwheel (C) by the number on the rear sprocket (S) and multiply by the size of the rear wheel, in inches (W). Or;

$$G = (C \div S) \times W$$

For a mountain bike W is almost always 26 inches, though some smaller bikes have 24inch wheels. The size will be marked on the side of the tyre.

A typical gear set of 24, 36, and 46 teeth chainrings and a 12-28 cluster has a range from 22 inches to 100 inches. The lowest gear is produced by the 24/28 combination, and the highest by the 46/12. At a comfortable pedalling rate of 80 rpm these produce speeds of 24mph and 5mph, respectively. To go faster or slower on a bike with this set-up you change your pedalling speed, though one of the reasons why bikes have gears is that human beings are only efficient within a fairly narrow range of pedalling rates, so if you find yourself climbing at under about 3mph you'd be more efficient if you got off and walked, or fitted a lower bottom gear.

Extreme gear systems are useful for some unusual applications. I know one tinkerer who runs a 14inch gear, achieved by using a modified 18-tooth sprocket as a chainring and running it through a 32-tooth rear sprocket. This gear allows him to climb ridiculously steep slopes, but he needs very good balance to stay on at under 2mph. At the other end of the scale, downhill racers like World Champion Greg Herbold run enormous 62/12 combinations on the steep, smooth descents of California's notorious Kamikaze run at Mammoth Mountain.

Cartridge bearing hubs

Cartridge bearings are complete sealed assemblies containing a cone, a cup, several ball bearings and a small quantity of grease. Unfortunately, because these bearings are designed to be sealed for life, there's little a home mechanic can do to service them. Removing the bearings would cause damage to their outer races, so any lubrication has to be done *in situ*. The only maintenance you can do yourself is periodic regreasing by removing the outer rubber seals and smearing grease into the bearing. Thankfully damaged bearings are reasonably easy to replace, and as there is no wear on the axle or hub, with occasional bearing replacement a hub will last you a long time.

To replace the bearings in SunTour XC-Comp and XC-Pro cartridge bearing hubs first get replacements from a SunTour dealer, who can obtain them from the importer, along with the necessary tools to fit them.

Take the lock-nuts, washers and bearing mountings (the bits where the cones would be on a cup and cone hub) off the axle and,

if this leaves one end in a bearing, tap it out with a rubber hammer. If you have to use a conventional hammer, put a nut over the end of the axle to prevent damage to the threads.

This leaves the bearings in the shell. Tap the old ones out with the SunTour tool and a length of steel bar (a drift). This of course destroys the bearings since the force needed to separate the bearing body from the shell is transmitted through the bearings, knocking dents into the balls and surfaces. However, since the reason you're taking the old

Special use gearing for downhill racing: a 42/52 chainset

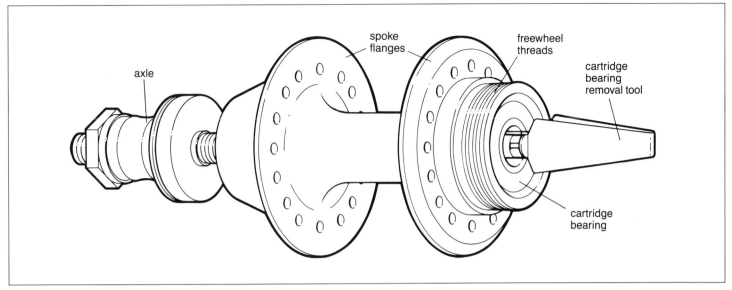

Labels: axle, spoke flanges, freewheel threads, cartridge bearing removal tool, cartridge bearing

Cartridge bearing hub

bearings out is because they've had it anyway, this doesn't matter.

To fit the new bearings use the special thick washers SunTour supply to push them in by the outer race only. This prevents you doing the kind of damage we've just mentioned. Fit a washer and bearing over the bearing mounting on the axle and put the other bearing, washer and mounting on the axle. Screw the bearing mounts together until the bearings have been pushed all the way into the hub shell.

Routine maintenance

I like to wipe a little grease on the exposed steel parts of my hubs, just to stop them rusting, but otherwise there's not much you can do in the way of day-to-day hub maintenance except service them as soon as they develop a problem. One modification I have seen on a few standard hubs is the fitting of a grease nipple in the middle of the hub shell, so that fresh grease can be easily pumped into the bearings, especially after they've been immersed. This is easiest to do on brand-new hubs, or when you're having your wheels rebuilt, and is the kind of a job an engineering-inclined mechanic should be able to do for you fairly easily.

9: Rims and spokes

In chapter 1, I jokingly referred to wheelbuilders as mechanics with a mystical mechanical aptitude that gives them an uncanny knack of mending bicycles by simply laying their hands on them. Well, it's kind of true: to learn how to build strong wheels takes quite some time. Fortunately, to learn the technique of fixing a wobbly wheel takes less. First you need to understand how a wheel stays together (or doesn't).

A bike wheel is a classic engineering structure, consisting of individually weak parts that together form a super-strong structure. Spokes (thin wire rods) support the rim, a rolled aluminium alloy extrusion, and connect it to the hub. Wheels gain their strength from the strength of the spokes in tension, and from the strength of the rim in compression. The spokes may be strong, but they can stretch, giving the wheel flexibility. Wheels survive the impacts that off-road riding subjects them to because their flexibility allows them to give a little, spreading the load across several spokes.

Let's take a more in-depth look at the various parts, before we see how to maintain them.

Rims

Rims are formed by forcing hot aluminium alloy through a die, to give a long length of aluminium bar with a variety of different cross-sections (*see below*). Lengths of this extrusion are then rolled and joined to form a hoop. How they're joined is reasonably academic: it may be by epoxy bonding, welding or rivetting. Every wheelbuilder has his own favourite type of rim.

Finally, the rim is completed by being drilled and eyeletted. Eyelets are ferrules that stop the spoke nipples pulling through the rim. Good rims have eyelets; cheap ones don't.

The cross-section of the rim is designed to give the wheel its strength. Listed in order of strength and lightness, the rim can have a

A box section rim

A twin channel rim

box-section bottom, twin channels, or two solid ribs in the bottom. In recent years, the average width of a rim has narrowed, yielding lighter wheels and improved tyre profiles, but the trade-off has been loss of lateral strength.

The best mountain bike rims come from Mavic, with Araya making a good production-bike rim.

Spokes

Spokes are lengths of rolled steel, formed with a bend at one end and a thread at the other for the nipple. They come in hundreds of different lengths, with several different types for specific uses.

A spoke's thickness is measured according to the standard wire gauge; for most purposes a plain 14 gauge (2mm thick) spoke is perfectly strong enough, and the even thicker $^{13}/_{14}$ gauge (2.3 – 2mm) ones are only really useful for expedition wheels or on tandems.

The spokes fitted to most mountain bikes are stainless steel, with a uniform 'plain gauge' profile, but high-end mountain bikes may

come with double- or single-butted spokes, with the end nearest the rim thinner than the hub end.

Increasingly we're seeing production bikes also coming out with double- or single-butted spokes, with the centre section between the nipple and the bend dropping down from 14 gauge to 16 gauge (2mm to 1.6mm). This isn't a daft idea, as the thinner spoke flexes more under load, allowing the wheel to absorb impacts better. Better still, it saves about a quarter of a pound in weight over a set of wheels. If you're having a new set of wheels built, ask for double-butted stainless steel spokes.

Spoke nipples

Spokes are tensioned to the rim with nipples, made from either chrome-plated brass or anodized aluminium. While aluminium nipples can save nearly an ounce of rotating weight, and are available in many attractive colours, they're ultimately not as strong as brass ones, and are really only suitable for race wheels. (The lighter the parts of the wheel furthest away from the hub are, the easier the bike is to accelerate.)

How a wheel works

The spoking pattern on a wheel means that the load on the wheel is spread across many spokes, instead of just one. The tension in these spokes keeps the wheel spinning in a circle – most of the time. When a wheel goes out of true, it's because a spoke or the rim has been permanently bent. Spokes hardly stretch at all, whereas rims are elastic up to a point, so they do stretch, and it's usually this that's the problem. If you imagine a wheel to be a tug-of-war between opposing teams of spokes, then it's obvious that to pull a rim over one way, you must

A front wheel showing 2
cross lacing

A rear wheel showing 3
cross lacing

tighten the spokes on one side, slacken them
on the other, or both. There's actually a bit
more to it than that, but for our purposes –
maintaining rims – it's all we need concern
ourselves with.

Truing a wheel

To true a wheel you don't need the full kit of
wheel jig and dishing tool, although if you
have them they do help. A spoke key is all
that's really needed, and you can use the
brake blocks to check for alignment.

There are two sorts of misalignment: *lateral*
or sideways bending, and *vertical* distortion
so that the rim is not quite circular. It's best
to deal with them in that order.

Find the section of the wheel that is knocked
out of line sideways, and see which way it's
bent. If there are several wobbles, work on
the worst one first. Tighten the spoke on the
opposite side of the rim at the point of most
error by half a turn. Back off the two
adjacent spokes on the other side by a
quarter turn, spin the wheel and see what
happens. If the rim is out along several
spokes, tighten by a quarter turn on the ones
further away from the worst point. Check
the error, and if it's still there, repeat the
process, but only tweaking the spokes
another half or quarter turn at a time. The
worst thing you can do is to haul the rim
back to the right position by putting five
turns in one spoke instead of distributing the
correction across several spokes.

If you've now got the wheel running so that
it doesn't wobble from side to side, check it
doesn't jump up and down. (This happens
when it's deformed so it is no longer truly
circular.) At a high point, tighten the spokes
half a turn on both sides of the rim, whereas

Correcting lateral misalignment

may be too bent to correct and will have to be replaced. If it has an obvious kink, it's probably a scrapper.

Replacing a rim

Even if you don't want to go the whole hog and build a wheel, if your rim needs replacing you can save the folks at the bike shop some time and save yourself some money by swapping the rim over yourself. Provided that the new rim takes the same size spokes (the folks at the shop will be able to tell you that), and that the wheel isn't incredibly old, you can transfer the spokes from your old bent rim to your new one.

Correcting vertical misalignment

if the rim dips down, then slacken the spokes by a half-turn at that point. This may have affected the side-to-side wobble again, so go back and check it again. Getting a wheel accurately circular again takes time and patience, and the only way is to do small amounts of correction several times to get the wheel back to normal. Sometimes a rim

A scrappable rim

the spokes off so that they're just held in place by a couple of turns of thread in the nipples. Now you can start taking each spoke out of the old rim completely, putting the nipple in the same hole in the other rim, and giving it a couple of turns to hold it in place. Once you've got all the spokes in the new holes, you can either decide to take it to your favourite bike shop for them to tension up to make a rideable wheel, or have a go yourself.

Replacing a rim

If it's a rear wheel, it's a good idea to remove the freehub sprockets or block before rebuilding it. By the way, it's impossible to remove a freewheel from a hub if it's not built into a wheel, as the rim is used to turn the hub when using a freewheel remover. The worst thing you can do is to cut the spokes from the wheel, leaving the freewheel in place.

Tape the new rim to the old one, making sure to get the orientation right, with the valve holes in the same place, and the offset spoke holes correctly positioned. Go all the way around your old wheel and loosen all

Tensioning

For building up a wheel from scratch, a jig and dishing tool are very useful, but I've built more than a couple of wheels in my bike frame. The first thing to do is to tighten all the spokes up to the same tension, and this is easily done by checking the amount of thread left at the top of the spoke nipple. Tighten them all so that the end of the spoke is level with the bottom of the screwdriver slot in the end of the nipple. If the spokes you're using are all the same length, which unfortunately isn't usually the case after several months' use, then the wheel should be pretty much spot on for tension. If it isn't, go around and try to get all the spokes to the same tension by plucking each one and listening for the same note. Add or remove tension accordingly.

If it's a rear wheel, the rim probably isn't in the centre of the rear triangle. This is because the position of the spokes on a rear wheel isn't the same as on a front one. The rim isn't usually directly between the spoke flanges, because the freewheel takes up room on one side of the hub, so that the spokes on that side are more vertical than the spokes on the other side. This is called 'dish', and what it means is that the spoke tension on the freewheel side of the wheel must be slightly greater than on the non-freewheel side. So you add a half-turn to all the spokes on the freewheel side, and take a quarter-turn off the others, to adjust the rim over to the centre. Then measure the gap between one side of the rim and the frame, take the wheel out, turn it round and replace it, and measure the gap again. If it's not the same, repeat the operation of adding half a turn and removing a quarter until it's right.

When you've got the wheel fairly round, you can start correcting vertical and lateral

A dished rear wheel. Note that the rim is central in the dropouts, but not in the middle of the spoke flanges

error in the same way that we described in the section on truing (see page 86).

The only real big stumbling block during all of this is the amount of tension the wheel should have in it. It's best to have another wheel to check the tension with. Too much, and the wheel can spontaneously fold into a crisp shape, destroying the rim, while too little can make the wheel fold when you ride off the first kerb. Again, if you're unsure, check with your local wheelbuilder.

Building from scratch

It's certainly possible to build strong wheels at home, and of all the maintenance aspects of working on your bike, I think it's the most rewarding, but you've got to spend lots of time getting it right. Whole books have been written on correct wheelbuilding theory! Once you've got the hang of how

Using a dishing tool to check for lateral misalignment

Starting from scratch with a long way to go – wheelbuilding is a long but rewarding job

adjusting the spoke tension affects the shape of a wheel, you can quickly pick up the extra skills needed to build complete strong wheels. All that's left to learn are the different lacing patterns for different uses and the correct amount of tension in each case. If you can find an experienced wheelbuilder to help you along, then great. By the time you reach this stage of experience you should have developed a good relationship with your local shop, and asking them nicely might be all that's required. If you can't find someone to help you, buy a cheap rim, hub and spokes and have a go yourself; it's certainly not as mystical as it's cracked up to be!

10: Headsets and forks

Headsets

Let's face it, mountain bike headsets get hammered. Steering bearing design is one department in which the mountain bike has not evolved significantly from the road bike and, consequently, this often-neglected bearing is one of the ones which needs most frequent attention. Nevertheless, it is possible to keep the little beast running smoothly with regular maintenance.

In the last couple of years mountain bike headsets have changed somewhat. The road bike size, which has a one inch diameter steering column, was the standard for almost a decade, but has now been almost completely replaced by two 'oversize' versions, Tioga's 1 ⅛in Avenger size and fisher's 1 ¼in Evolution size. These headsets have more and larger bearings than the road bike size and have gone some of the way towards making headsets more durable and reliable. Nevertheless, the headset hasn't changed at all in engineering terms, it's just bigger. Whether this was necessary or not is still an item of contention in some circles, but there's no doubt at all that the 'oversize' types are now the twin industry standards. They won't, I suspect, go the way of STI on top line bikes and disappear from whence they came, because, although their theoretical advantages may not be necessary,

Pre-race checking. Tighten that headset!

they don't have any disadvantages except the necessity of adding four more spanners to the average pro mechanic's tool kit.

After I wrote about headsets in *Mountain Biking UK* a couple of years ago, I got a letter from a reader asking why no-one used taper roller bearings in them, since these have a much greater bearing contact area and would therefore be much more durable. The simple answer was that standard bearings are so much more tolerant of slight errors in the alignment of bearing mounting surfaces that it was much cheaper for manufacturers to use them, than to produce frames and forks that were accurately enough engineered for a taper-roller headset to work. Since then, Klein's Attitude and Adroit superbikes, which use large aircraft control bearings that cannot be adjusted in the headset, have shown that alternative headset designs *can* work, and I wonder if we aren't waiting for a leap forward in headset design like the ones that have occurred in gears and brakes recently. It's about the only bike part that hasn't been radically redesigned.

Anyway, on with the business at hand. The topic of headsets splits neatly into **problem diagnosis, maintenance and lubrication** and **replacement,** so we'll take them in that order.

Problem diagnosis

Aside from the issue of the three different sizes, headsets come in three types: stiff (too tight), stiff (bearing damage) and loose. Oh, and working right. *Sutherland's Handbook for Bicycle Mechanics* lists eleven different possible problems and causes for malcontent headsets of which the last is: 'Poor quality headset. Some just aren't designed to work.' In our workshop these are known as type eleven headsets and can only be cured by replacement.

For other problems, less radical cures exist if the trouble is caught early. If, however, you ride around for two months on a loose headset, don't expect much sympathy from your local shop if it will not run smoothly when you get around to tightening it. Indeed, this goes for all bearings – an ounce of timely prevention can save you pounds of expensive cures.

A loose headset will manifest itself as a shaking or juddering of the forks as you brake and can be easily checked for by holding the front brake on hard, and rocking the bike backwards and forwards. If the headset clicks or rocks from one position to another, then it's loose.

A tight headset will not turn smoothly in the head tube, or will exhibit 'click stop' steering. Often the only permanent cure for such units is replacement, but a temporary cure is to replace the caged balls with loose ones, as detailed below.

An over-tight headset can also produce an entertaining mode of steering failure that engineers call 'capsize', which occurs when the bike is unable to turn as much as you need it to when you lean into a turn, with the result that you fall off. Fortunately this tends to be a low-speed problem, but if you feel that your bike isn't handling right in tight, tricky, slow situations, check the headset. The most serious headset fault is when it is loose or properly adjusted when pointing directly forward, but becomes tight when turned to the side. This is a symptom of a bent steerer tube and indicates that the forks, or at least the steerer, need replacing.

Tools

The only essential tools are a good pair of thin headset spanners the right size for your headset – Park, Shimano, Campag or the slightly cheaper Leda or Tacx ones. These are not cheap, but do have bottom bracket tools on the other ends, so they kill two birds with one stone.

Old-style, 1in, road bike size headsets need 32mm spanners, Tioga 1 ⅛in need 36mm jobs, and Fisher Evolution 1 ¼in headsets require 40mm spanners. The problem of the availability of these tools, which plagued the early days of oversize headsets, has now eased, and any bike shop should be able to get them for you.

Maintenance and lubrication

If your headset is just in need of adjustment, then there's no need to do more than tighten the locknut and top race cup against each other. Loosen the headset by unscrewing the locknut anti-clockwise, holding the top race with the other spanner. The top cup should then be adjusted by hand so that the forks turn freely and without play, then held in place with one spanner while the locknut is tightened with the other. If a headset will not tighten no matter what you do with it, the fork crown race may be loose; if so it will need replacing. It's also possible that the fork crown race mounting has been cut too small and will need building up with brass and re-cutting. This is a job for a frame builder.

Another reason why a headset will not tighten even though the locknut appears to tighten against something, is that the steering column is too long and the locknut is locking against the top of the steerer rather than the top race. If this is the case it can be diagnosed by dismantling the headset (*see below*) to remove the locknut and comparing the height of the locknut to the height of the steerer remaining above the race. If there is more steerer than locknut, fit a spacer.

Catching problems before they become serious is the key to day-to-day maintenance of headsets. I am still running the original Deore headset that came with my Dave Yates three years ago, and regular dismantling, cleaning and bearing replacement has kept it smooth as a baby's bum.

Dismantling

To do more than merely adjust the headset, for example to lubricate it, it will need dismantling. The first step is to disconnect the front brake then remove the handlebar and stem from the frame, to allow access to the guts of the headset. Loosen the stem by unscrewing the 6mm Allen key bolt in the middle of it anti-clockwise. Tap the bolt down with a hammer and a piece of wood to release the expander or wedge from the

First slacken the Allen bolt

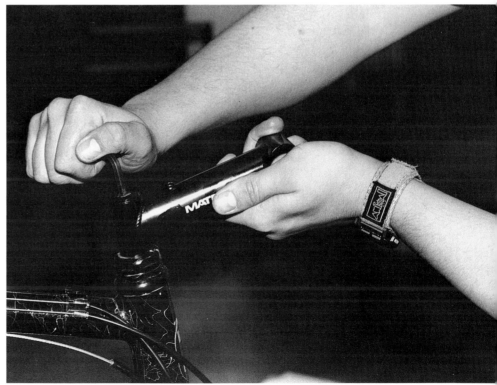

steerer. If the stem still won't move try soaking it in penetrating oil (LPS-1, WD-40) for a while before trying again.

If this fails, it's time to take it down to the bike shop for the judicious application of some brute force. The first line of attack is to turn the bike upside down in a workshop stand, fill the inside of the steerer with penetrating oil and leave it to marinade overnight. Then, clamp the fork crown in a vice and attempt to turn the bars, perhaps with a long tube over the end of the bar for extra leverage.

If *this* doesn't work, you usually have to take the decision to write off the stem, saw off the top of it and use heat or chemical means to remove the lump of stem which remains. Alloy stems can be dissolved out with caustic soda, steel stems heated till they submit. A

thoroughly seized stem is likely to be unusable by the time it's out; the forks usually survive, though I have seen road bike forks bend under the force needed to free a really recalcitrant stem.

With the stem out, the headset is dismantled by loosening the locknut and top cup and unscrewing them from the steerer. The fork can then be lowered from the frame. Remove the caged bearings from the headset and take them to the shop with you when you buy replacements, to make sure you get the right size of loose balls. Remove the rubber seals from the top and bottom parts of the headset and put them somewhere safe, noting which goes where and which way up. Clean all the bearing surfaces and inspect them for wear or pitting. If any parts are worn you'll probably need to replace the whole headset, since spares are both hard to find and ridiculously expensive.

Headset assembly

To reassemble the headset you'll need about 55 5/32in ball bearings for a road-size headset, and enough bearings of the appropriate size for an oversize headset. Headsets are one area of a bike where caged bearings are simply not justifiable. Since a headset just takes impact loads, and does not have to turn much, it needs as many bearings as possible to maximise the bearing surface. In addition, oversize headsets use larger bearings than road bike units because the increase in surface area of the bearings increases the total bearing surface faster than the larger diameter reduces it. Most 1⅛in oversize headsets use 7/32in balls, 1in and 1¼in Shimano Deore XT headsets take ¼in balls, as do most other 1¼in headsets. When you buy replacement loose balls, get about twice as many as there are in the

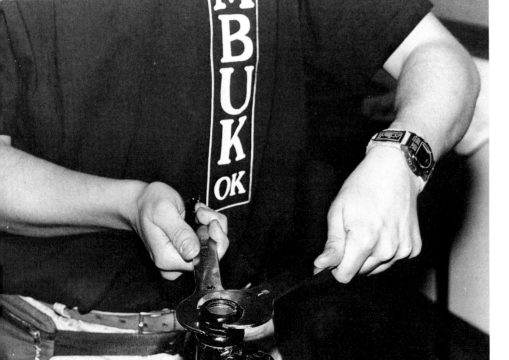
Then remove the locknut

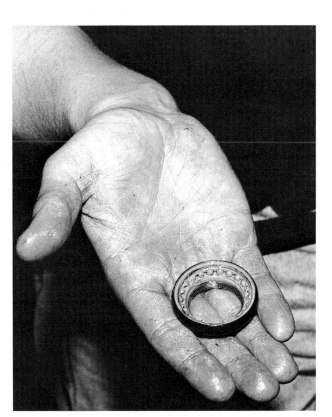

A 1⅛ in headset race

Headset replacement

I have to say that I consider this a job best left to a bike shop. However, if you must know how to do it, here goes. Dismantle the headset as above. Remove the fork crown race from the fork by lifting it off with a hammer and punch. Tap alternately each of the sides which overlap the fork crown until the race is free of its mounting. To remove the cups from the frame, tap them out from the inside with a hammer and a piece of half-inch cylindrical steel bar with clean, sharp edges. If the edge you tap the thin cup with is burred, it will slip off, making the job significantly more difficult. Move round the point at which you tap so that the cup comes out evenly.

cages. Don't worry if they don't all fit; headsets vary and there's an allowance in that number for the inevitable one or two that fall on the floor and disappear!

Smear a thick layer of grease into the bottom race cup and place the bearings into it. There should be enough grease to hold them in place. Replace the seal in the cup. Repeat the procedure with the top race cup, since you want it ready to put in place when you insert the forks. Now insert the forks in the frame, taking care not to dislodge any balls from the bottom race cup, and screw the top race cup down on the forks. Shimano Deore series headsets have the top race cup installed in the frame rather than as a screw-on unit, so the balls sit in this cup and care must also be taken to avoid dislodging them.

Removing a top headset race with a rocket tool

If you are likely to do this job often, which means that you are setting up either a club workshop or a bike shop, Park make a rather useful tool which slips into the head tube and allows you to evenly knock out the headset cups. Its four flared parts look like fins from a rocket in a fifties sci-fi movie; it is sensibly called a rocket tool and makes the job of fully dismantling a headset much easier.

Take the old headset and the forks with you when you go to buy a replacement. Headsets differ in the size of the fork crown race mounting and, while most road bike size ones are 26.4mm, a few 27mm ones are still about. 1⅛in headsets have 30.0mm fork crown race mounting, while 1 ¼in units are 33.0mm. The fork crown race is intended to be a tight 'interference' fit on the fork crown. If it drops on easily it is too large.

Stack height

The other potential source of fitting hassle is the issue of 'stack height'. This is the amount of extra steering column length that the headset needs, over and above the length of the head tube. Shimano headsets tend to have very low stack heights and can therefore be replaced only with other Shimano headsets. One Japanese bike manufacturer, Bridgestone, finds this so annoying that they insert a wide spacer into the Shimano headsets on their bikes so that any headset

A rocket tool. Used for headset cup removal

96

can be fitted. It is essential to get a headset with the same stack height as the original one, or spacers to get the locknut to tighten if you are fitting a Shimano headset to a bike that didn't have one. I don't suggest that you should cut down the steerer to make the new headset fit, because you would then limit your choice of replacement headsets forever.

To illustrate the point, road size Shimano headsets typically have stack heights of around 33mm, whereas most headsets are some five or six millimetres higher than this. That few millimetres is difficult to put back once it has been cut off!

Reassembly

To fit the crown race, tap it gently home with the steel bar you used to remove the cups, taking care *not* to tap the bearing surface, but the flat top edge of the race. A better tool is a piece of tube which fits over the steerer closely so that it cannot slip off. I use a piece of 1.2mm thick, 28.6mm wide Tange ATB seat tube which I salvaged from a written-off Saracen Tufftrax. This tool also allows you to fit the crown race by the subtle technique of banging the end of the tube on the floor, getting round the problem of how to hold the forks while tapping the race on.

Fitting the cups is best done with a Park, VAR or Campag headset press. Unfortunately they have three-figure price tags and are beyond the means of anyone but a bike shop. The alternative is to gently tap in the cups with a hammer, placing a wooden block between hammer and cup to stop the cup getting damaged and spread the load. When the cups and crown race are in place the headset can be reassembled as above.

Forks

The fork is the first thing that gets mangled in a front end collision. A properly designed mountain bike will have a fork that fails before the frame, since forks are less expensive than frames, and easier to replace. In recent years some forks have become so over-designed that a frame will fold while the fork cheerfully sits there and takes it; not a sensible design. Unfortunately it is easier to design a super-strong fork than a super-strong frame.

A headset press in place

A bent fork will manifest itself by causing the headset to become stiff when turned a long way to the side, even though it is smooth within a few degrees of straight ahead. While it is possible to straighten a crash-damaged fork with lots of brute force, this is an emergency, get-you-home measure, and a bent fork should be replaced immediately. A fork that has been bent and then straightened will be severely weakened and could break at any time. It should not be ridden.

To fit a new fork, it first needs to be cut to length. Either measure it against the original fork or assemble it into the frame, fit the top race and allow sufficient threads for the locknut. Mark the point where the fork needs to be cut by making the beginning of a saw cut.

Dismantle the fork from the frame and screw a top race onto the thread so that the cutting mark is at the top of the race. Use the race as a guide when cutting the forks down, so that you get a straight cut. When you've cut off the excess steerer, file the top of it smooth and unscrew the race from the fork. This will push the thread at the top of the steerer back into shape, allowing you to screw a new one on. Clean any metal filings off the fork and – especially – the crown race before reassembling the headset.

If there is insufficient thread on the steerer to enable you to trim it to length without running out of thread, you will need to get extra thread cut on the fork. This really is a job for an experienced bike shop mechanic. Cutting fork threads involves using a special tool, and takes about twenty minutes per

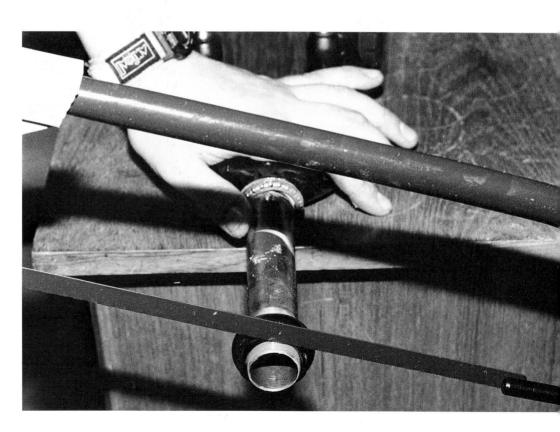

Cutting a steerer tube to length. Thread a headset race onto the fork to reform the thread when you've cut it

Tim Davies using the Accu-Trax fork

inch if you know what you're doing. If you don't know what you're doing you will produce a ragged thread that won't take a headset and will ruin the fork. Far safer to put the job into sure hands and pay for the reassurance that it's their problem if anything goes wrong.

Fork choice

Mountain bike forks have been the subject of intensive development in the last couple of years. Testing done by Brant Richards at MBUK on a wide variety of aftermarket forks produced some interesting results. For a start, it doesn't seem to matter whether a fork is straight or curved. A fork is a cantilevered beam, and how it gets from the crown to the hub seems to make no difference to the way the fork absorbs shock. Since most mountain bike forks are pretty rigid in a straight line, and tyres are not, most of the shock absorption in a standard front end seems to go on in the tyre.

What matters more is the fork's resistance to torsional deflection, and this is determined by the size and configuration of the fork blades themselves. In short, wide diameter fork blades resist twisting better than thin ones and therefore give better handling, a point to bear in mind when choosing new forks.

Suspension

Only a few suspension forks are currently available, notably Rock Shox, the Marzocchi Star Fork, Manitou suspension fork (now made by Answer) and the first prototypes of Pace Research's RC-35 fork. All these appear to work, and give a considerable

Adjusting the pressure in a pair of Rock Shox hydraulic suspension forks

improvement in comfort and control, especially at high speed. Most of the medals in the downhill and cross-country events at the first World Mountain Bike Championships were taken home by riders using Rock Shox, proving that suspension forks work and provide a significant competitive advantage. At the moment Rock Shox are generally considered to be the best suspension fork, simply because they have been around long enough for their designer, Paul Turner, to have ironed out most of the bugs.

Though all the suspension forks available may look similar, they are divided according to what method they use to suspend the bike and rider. Rock-Shox and Marzocchi forks use an air spring and oil damper to provide the shock absorbing medium, with the Pace RC-35's and Manitou forks using elastomer foam rubbers. Oils and springs allow much more fine tuning of the suspension, but elastomers are light, cheap and easy to service. Over the short travel of a mountain bike suspension fork, typically 2in or less, the rubbers work well.

11: Pedals

If there's a part on a mountain bike which should cause frequent problems, it's the pedals. No other moving part of the bike gets as near to the ground, or immersed in streams, puddles and liquid mud as frequently as the pedal bearings, and pedals are often the first part of the bike to land when you take a tumble.

It's no surprise, then, that cyclo-crossers and some mountain bike racers use the cheapest, lightest pedals around, Lyotard alloy rat-traps. These are so inexpensive that they can be treated as expendable. Indeed, I know a couple of mountain bikers who've tried them and soon stopped using them because they are too expendable. Hit them hard enough on a rock and they practically explode!

Most mid-priced mountain bikes come with indifferent to reasonably good pedals, and it's worth keeping them in good condition.

As far as maintenance goes, mountain bike pedals range from easily serviceable to forget-it-and-buy-new-ones. Most can be dismantled, regreased and reassembled fairly easily, though I know at least one pro mechanic who hates pedals because their bearings are not simple to adjust. Nevertheless, with a little patience you can keep the little beasts running sweetly. The very cheapest pedals cannot be serviced at all, and the only thing to do if such pedals malfunction is to junk them and buy good replacements.

As usual for bearings the symptoms of pedals in need of TLC are sticking, grinding, clicking or looseness. Often these will manifest as clicking noises while you pedal and you should check your pedals first as a possible source of hassle before checking that your bottom bracket and chainring bolts are tight. A well-adjusted pedal will spin freely but exhibit no looseness when rocked against the crank. To check this, grab the pedal in one hand and the crank in the other. If the pedal body moves relative to the crank or doesn't spin easily, then it's repair time!

Pedals usually have flats where they screw into the crank for a special, long 15mm spanner. Lyotard pedals are 17mm. Most sets of bottom bracket tools include a 15mm pedal spanner on the opposite end of the fixed cup spanner, but specific 15mm pedal spanners can be had from bike shops. The right hand pedal is right-hand threaded and so unscrews anti-clockwise and the left pedal is left hand threaded and unscrews clockwise. Some pedals have 6mm Allen key holes in the end of the axle which is behind the crank, and can thus be removed with a long 6mm Allen key. It's easy to remember which way to turn the spanner or Allen key, as the top of the tool always turns towards

Removing a pedal from a crank arm

the back of the bike.

If the pedals are stuck, give the end of the axle a good dousing in a thin penetrating oil such as WD40 or LPS1 and leave it for a few hours. A sharp tap from a hammer on the spanner may be needed to loosen the pedal, but if it still won't come off take it into your local bike shop and make it their problem; they may be able to sort it out by more drastic methods.

One extreme technique for removing a pedal is to take the entire crank off the axle and hold it in a vice to gain extra leverage. Make sure you use soft jaws to avoid damage to the crank. Probably the ultimate sanction is to heat up the end of the crank (gently!) with a brazing torch. The aluminium crank will expand more quickly than the steel axle, allowing the axle to move. Neither of these techniques are possible if you don't have the right tools, and brazing torches are not the sort of thing you find in the average home workshop.

If you have managed to get a pedal totally seized in the crank, bear in mind that it may simply be impossible to get it out, and it's not a dealer's fault if attempting to do so wrecks the crank. Pedals seize because corrosion causes the aluminium of the crank to expand and trap the axle, since aluminium oxide (the product of corrosion) is much bulkier than aluminium. Aluminium oxide is also much weaker than aluminium, just as rust is weaker than steel, and when the axle finally does move it is not unusual for it to sheer the remnants of the thread in the axle. A new crank is the only solution; the pedal usually survives.

Dustcaps

Having removed the pedal, you now have to remove the dustcap to get at the bearings. This is usually an awkward process. How awkward depends on the type of pedal; expensive pedals tend to be easier to service than cheap ones.

Dustcap removal usually involves simple brute force. On most mountain bike pedals the dustcap is prised off by slipping a thin-bladed screwdriver underneath it. This sounds easy enough, but if the fit is particularly tight it can be extremely difficult to get the dustcap off without destroying it. It makes life easier if you remove the cage from the pedal, if you can. Deore and Deore

Removing the pedal cage. Clean the Allen bolts to avoid rounding the hexagonal sockets

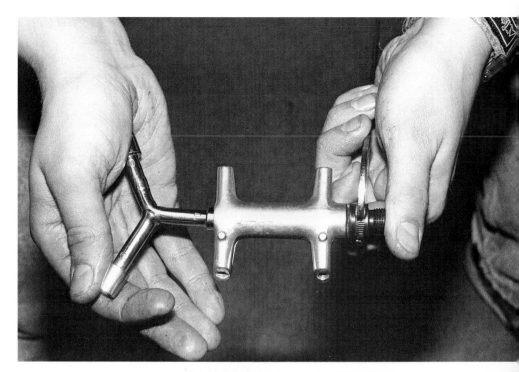

XT pedals allow this, giving access to the dustcap, as do some recent SR and Taiwanese pedals but this is not possible on cheaper Shimano pedals. Fortunately the cut away design of most current pedals allows you to get at the dustcap without removing the cage. Some pedals have dustcaps that are removed with a tool such as an Allen key or a peg spanner.

Dismantling

Having got off the dustcap, you now need to dismantle the bearings themselves. Inside the pedal you can see the heads of two nuts. These are commonly 10mm and 12mm, although other sizes are not unknown and you'll basically need a set of small metric socket spanners to be sure of getting exactly the right size.

To remove the outer nut (locknut) hold the axle with a 6mm Allen key or a pedal spanner and unscrew it anti-clockwise. Do not lose this nut! It's usually an odd thread for its size and replacements can be very difficult to come by. There may be a tab washer under the locknut which will need a bit of perseverance to remove since it tends to catch on the threads; try waggling it off with a screwdriver if it won't easily fall off.

The cone is the easiest bit to remove. Most have hexagonal ends and can be removed with a socket spanner. If a socket spanner won't fit (there may not be enough space), use a large flat-bladed screwdriver to hold the cone while you turn the axle from the other end. When the cone is out the axle can be

Removing the cone with a large screwdriver

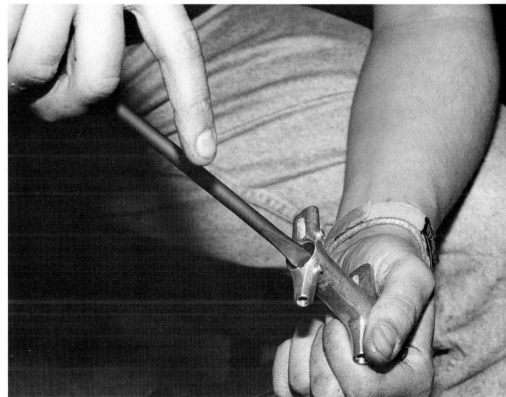

removed. Clean everything with solvent and examine the bearing surfaces. Replace anything which is worn and replace the bearing balls anyway (you'll probably loose half of them when you take the axle out). Pedal bearing balls are typically 1/8in and there are about 25 per pedal. Deore and Deore XT bearings are 3/32in; pretty damn tiny. If the bearing surfaces in the pedal body are worn there's no alternative but to replace the pedal. Since they're only available in pairs a bit of preventive maintenance can be a major money saver.

Reassembly

Pedals are the bearings which are most likely to get immersed in water, or at least splashed frequently. The best way to protect them from this is to pack the bearings with lots of thick waterproof grease. Boat trailer wheel grease is available from marine supply shops and is ideal for this application, as well as for the hubs, headset and pedal bearings of any bike that gets regularly immersed.

Smear plenty of grease on the bearing cups in the pedal body and put the bearings in. Put more grease on top of them and reassemble the pedal. If there is a seal on the inboard end of the axle put it into the pedal body and drop the axle through. There should be enough grease in the bearing so that it oozes out of the crank end of the pedal. Next screw the cone down onto the outboard bearings until it touches them. Push on the tab washer and screw on the locknut.

The bearings of Deore and XT pedals are buried in the pedal body and can be very

Replace the bearings with the help of a thin-bladed screwdriver

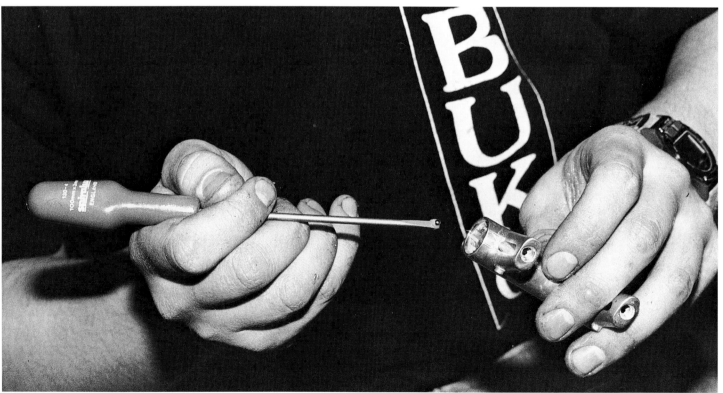

awkward to get at. Fine tweezers or a long, thin magnetic screwdriver are the order of the day for lifting bearings in and out of the confined space of a Deore or XT pedal body. Shimano could make our lives a bit easier by making these excellent pedals a bit more user-serviceable.

Incidentally, I recently discovered a way of packing pedal bearings with grease without dismantling them. I was assembling a Trek 850 for a member of the MBUK staff (yes, guess who gets to do all the bike maintenance jobs round here!) when I realised that the push-in plastic dustcaps could be used to squeeze grease into the bearing. Fill the outer bearing with grease so that it comes right up to the edge of the pedal, fill the dustcap with grease and fit the cap into the pedal. Spin the axle a couple of times to allow the grease to penetrate the pedal, and repeat as many times as necessary to squeeze grease out of the inboard bearing.

A more advanced version of this technique would be to drill or punch small holes in a pair of spare dustcaps and use a syringe or grease gun, like the SunTour or Pedro's ones, to inject grease though the spare dustcaps, then re-fit the original ones. Unfortunately, this assumes you can get spare dustcaps, and often you can't for any but the most famous major-name pedals. For dealers, obtaining and stocking pedal dustcaps, which do occasionally get knocked off and lost, was a serious hassle in the days when road bikes came equipped with a narrow range of pedals. With literally dozens of models of mountain bike pedals out there, it's become a nightmare, so bear with your dealer if they just can't get you a dust cap for the Dai Yung pedals on your Rubberstamped Comp!

Adjustment

This is where pedals are interesting and slightly irritating. Unlike all other bike bearings it's not possible to hold the cone while tightening the locknut, though pedal manufacturers must have some cool tools that allow them to do this. Fortunately the tab washer, if there is one, does prevent some cone movement, but not all of it. Pedal adjustment therefore has to be done by a process of trial and error involving setting the cone slightly loose and tightening the locknut until the cone beds down where you want it. To do this, use a flat-bladed screwdriver to tweak the position of the cone, tighten the locknut and spin the pedal.If it is loose, slacken the locknut and screw the cone down a small amount (⅛-¼ of a turn) and retighten. If it's tight, slacken the locknut and bearing off similarly. Patience is the key here, as you may need to repeat the process several times before it comes right.

Push or screw the dustcap back in and replace the pedal body if you removed it. Grease the pedal threads, screw them back into the cranks and *voila!* you're away again.

Toeclips

There are a couple of things to remember when fitting toeclips and straps. Almost all mountain bikes use plastic toeclips because steel ones disintegrate rapidly in off-road use. You only have to step on a steel clip a few times for it to become fatigued and break. Choose clips that are the right length for your shoes or boots; they should position the ball of your foot over the pedal axle.

There are two ways to stop straps from pulling through the pedal when you pull them tight. The traditional way is to twist the strap as it goes through the pedal cage, so that it cannot easily move through the pedal, but a useful alternative is to use a plastic cable tie, available from electronics shops, to attach the strap to the back of the pedal cage so that it lies flush against it. This prevents the strap from acting as a mud platform.

Clipless pedals

For a couple of years a few mountain bike racers have used Look or Time pedals which engage special cleats on the sole of the shoe. These systems were intended for road bikes and have not been widely used off-road because they tend not to work well in mud, are all but impossible to ride unless the shoe is clipped into the top of the pedal and the raised cleat makes walking in them awkward. British mountain bike star David Baker and US Team Ritchey rider Don Myrah nevertheless rode Look pedals with special aluminium cleats to numerous successes, but this system just wasn't suitable for the majority of riders.

Towards the end of 1990, Shimano introduced a clipless pedal system for mountain bikes. SPD (Shimano Pedalling Dynamics) consists of a double-sided pedal and a shoe with a recessed cleat.

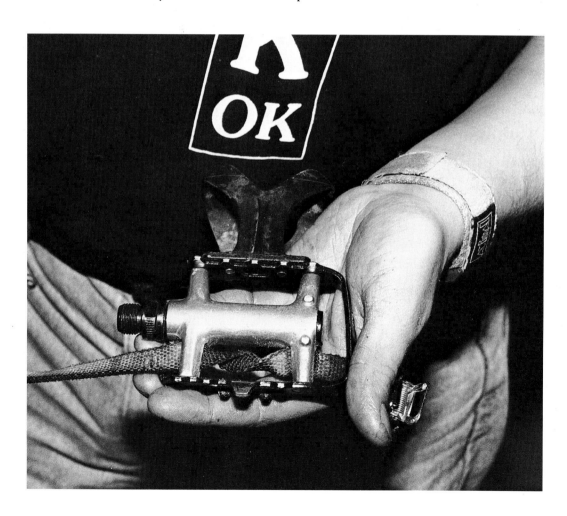

Twist the toestraps to stop them pulling through

A Shimano SPD clipless pedal. The first high performance mountain bike clipless pedal system, it gave a new feeling of freedom and movement to off-road riders – highly recommended

The system works in virtually all conditions; ice and snow clog it up, but it shrugs off mud and has been a major success with racers and affluent recreational riders. At the time of writing it's not cheap, but less expensive versions should become available over the next twelve months.

The maintenance requirements of SPD are simple. Wash the mud out of them thoroughly after each ride. The springs which engage the locking mechanism are clearly visible and should be kept well-lubricated. The bearings are removed as a complete axle cartridge, with a special tool (TL-PD40). The cartridge is then serviced in exactly the same way as a conventional pedal bearing.

Pedal selection

Over the last few years mountain bike pedals have undergone the same racing-driven evolution as almost all parts of the off-road bike. Originally mountain bike pedals were straight adaptations of BMX pedals, with larger threads on the ends to fit the TA road bike triple cranksets the pioneers of mountain biking used. These 'bear-trap' pedals were huge, heavy and relied for their grip on wicked-looking sharp teeth in their steel outer cages. These teeth afforded

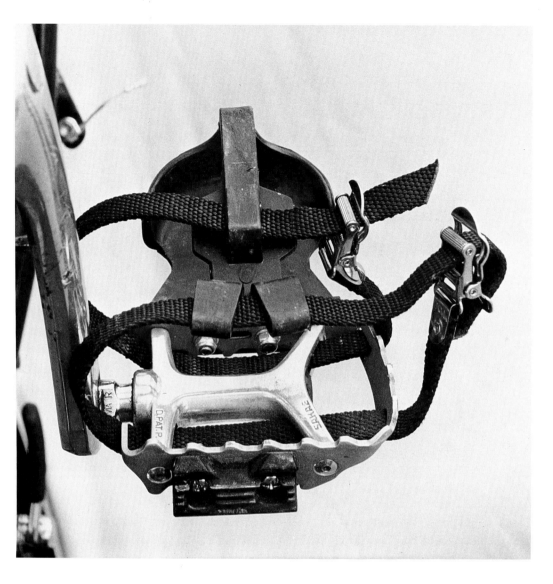

SR Low Fat pedal with Kona Joe's clips

amazing grip on soft-soled trainers or waffle-soled boots, but if you did slip off they dug great gouges out of your shins. Cheerfully known as 'bear tracks', they hurt. Lots.

Ten years later mountain bike pedals resemble nothing so much as beefed-up road bike pedals with a few teeth for grip. The BMX pedal of yesteryear is almost dead. For most applications the 'toothy road pedal' design works excellently. For racing and fast recreational riding pedals like Shimano's

Deore and XT models, SunTour's XC series and SR's Low Fat models offer light weight, high ground clearance and reliability, plus the ability to take toe clips easily. You can even use them with cleated cyclo-cross shoes for ultimate performance in racing.

Nevertheless, there are a few of the old-style pedals still about, and they have some useful applications. If you just can't get on with toeclips hunt out a set of 1988 Shimano Deore XT bear traps or original SunTour

XC-II pedals. These provide loads of grip, even without toeclips. Touring mountain bikers tend to prefer these pedals because their large surfaces make them more comfortable with hiking boots, which are still preferred to mountain bike shoes for trips which may involve long walking sections.

For racing, as mentioned above, clipless pedals seem to be taking over even more rapidly than they did on the road. How quickly they become accepted by recreational mountain bikers will depend on how soon budget versions become available,

since the system currently costs around £150 for pedals and shoes.

The advantage of double-sided clipless pedals is the speed with which you can get in and out of them, compared to conventional systems, and the security with which they hold your feet. I suspect that the SPD system, or something like it, will be the accepted standard in about three years time; if Shimano produce versions which are cheap enough that it does not drastically increase the price of a bike to have them fitted, this may happen even sooner.

12 : Bars and stems

Bars and stems have come a long way since the early days of mountain biking, when one-piece units called 'Bullmoose' bars were used; these weren't either light or adjustable, so as the mountain bike developed, the riders demanded a handlebar/stem unit that was adjustable. Manufacturers briefly used cast or forged alloy stems, but today most bikes use a stem made from steel, aluminium or sometimes titanium tubing, welded together to form a light, strong and stable support for the handlebars. The bars themselves are available in several different materials, but for the most part also come in aluminium or steel. Bar-ends are incredibly useful bolt-on extras that offer a much more powerful and comfortable climbing position on- or off-road.

Selecting handlebars

There are several reasons you may want to change your handlebars. You may have bent them in a crash, you may be uncomfortable about their position, or you may wish to replace them for a lighter model. This last reason isn't as daft as it may sound, as many production bikes have incredibly heavy bars, and switching models can sometimes save as much as 4 to 5oz.

Bars aren't usually straight lengths of tubing, they have a bend at each side of the stem of between 0 and 12°, with 5° being the most common. To allow the bends to pass through the stem, the diameter of the clamp is larger than the diameter of the part of the bar where the bend is. Most mountain bike stems have a 1in diameter stem clamp, with the bars having a 7⁄8in section for the brake levers, grips and thumbshifters to clamp to.

There are two ways of making the bars fit the stem. One type, called 'Bulge Bars', has the centre section of the bar enlarged to fit the stem; the other uses a curved spacer, called a shim, to make the small-diameter handlebar fit. Recently production bikes fitted with 'Big Bulge' bars have hit the market; these bars have a 1 1⁄8in centre section. They claim lighter weight and greater strength, but without the aftermarket backup they give users a problem when replacing the stem or bars. In the future these may well become more popular, but for the time being I'm not convinced.

Replacing bars is a case of 'you pays your money and takes your choice', with materials as wide-ranging as carbon steel and carbon fibre. The more expensive bars weigh less, are stronger and offer better shock-absorbing characteristics. Great bars come from Answer, and Tioga offer good value.

The good old days of bullmoose bars

112

Answer Hyperlite bars and a Ritchey stem

Fitting handlebars

To fit new bars you fairly obviously have to take off your old ones. The biggest problem isn't getting the brakes or shifters off, it's removing the grips. I usually stick a thin-bladed screwdriver between the grip and the handlebar, then squirt in water from a water bottle. After much squidging and tugging around they usually come flying off. The other alternative is simply to cut the grips off and replace them too. Loosen the brake and

gear lever bar-clamps and slide them off the ends of the bars, then by loosening the handlebar clamp you can slide the old bars out. To fit the new ones, simply reverse the procedure. Here's a useful tip for installing bars without scratching them. Take the clamp bolt out of the clamp and thread it in again upside-down from the bottom. Put a small coin in the slot in the stem so that the bolt pushes against it, ensuring the coin doesn't protrude into the clamp, then tighten the bolt up. This springs the clamp apart a

little further and gives you more room to manoeuvre.

Replace the control levers in the position you find most comfortable, which for most people means angling them down at 30 – 45°. Fitting the grips and getting them to stay there is tricky; foam grips usually come with their own glue, but for rubber grips I use large amounts of hairspray! Before riding the bike, make sure the adhesive holding the grips is dry and that they aren't going to fly off. Even more crucial, check that the brakes have been reconnected properly.

Use hairspray to stick grips back on

115

Trimming the bars

Small riders, especially women, aren't comfortable spreadeagled in the crucifix position that the bars on production bikes tend to dictate. Don't imagine for a moment that you have to keep your handlebars the same width as you bought them; most riders run a bar 20 – 22in wide. Slide the controls and grips on your bike in, and try it for a few days before lopping the ends of your bars off... it's harder to increase a cut-down handlebar's length than it is to reduce it! For cutting bars down, you can use a hacksaw or a pipe-cutter. If you hacksaw the ends off, clean up the burrs with a file before putting the grips on. I don't have to tell you to trim equal amounts off each end of the bar, and not to shorten them at just one side, do I?

Selecting stems

If you're unhappy with the shape, weight, colour or taste of your current stem, then replace it. As with handlebars, there's a

Using a pipe-cutter to shorten handlebars

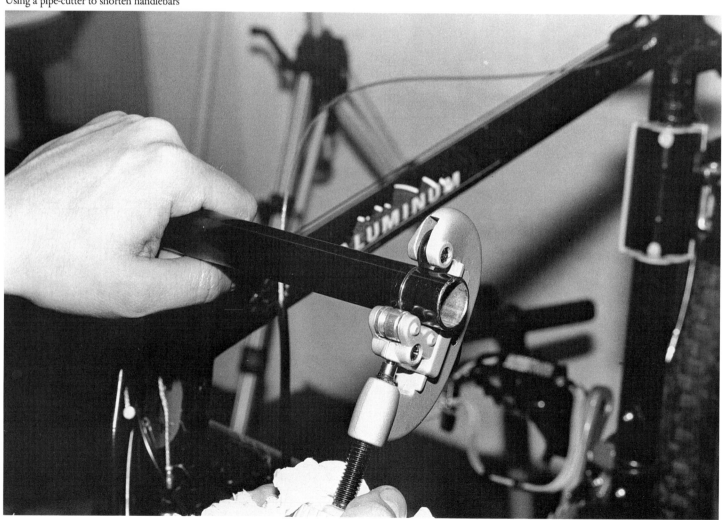

116

dizzying array of possibilities on the market, from steel-welded models such as the Tioga T-Bone to the shock-absorbing, pivoting Offroad Flexstem.

Riders with oversize headsets obviously need to look for corresponding oversize stems to fit in the fork, though shims are available if you really want to fit a regular-size stem into an oversize fork. There are stems of many different sizes on the market; a stem is measured in terms of its *reach*, the horizontal distance from the centreline of the quill to the clamp centre, and its *rise*, the vertical distance from the point of minimum height in the fork to the clamp centre.

Stems differ not only in size, but also in their method of routeing the front brake cable. Some models have internal rollers, while some have external rollers, a fixed stop or no mounting at all. Internal rollers have fallen out of favour because there is no way of seeing if the cable is correctly positioned on the roller, or if it's being frayed out of sight of the user. If you use an internal-roller stem, check the cable carefully every couple of weeks, or replace the cable stop with a headset-mounted hanger. Salsa, Answer and Ritchey make great stems, with Tioga again making good value replacement models.

Fitting stems

If you want to replace your stem, you'll have to remove your bars first, though if you're cunning you should only have to disturb the grips and brake levers on one side.

A stem is held in place by the action of the wedge tightening against the chamfer on the bottom of the quill in the steerer tube. To loosen the stem you need to 'unlock' these two components. Slacken the Allen bolt in the quill a couple of turns, then tap the bolt

After slackening the Allen bolt, hit it with a hammer

with a hammer, protecting it with a piece of wood. This should knock the wedge down in the steerer tube, releasing the stem and allowing you to remove it from the fork. After having released the front brake, grip the front wheel between your knees, and twist the handlebars from side to side while pulling upwards. The stem should slide out of the forks easily. If it doesn't, then you'll need to squirt some WD40 or similar penetrating oil down the gap between the stem and the steerer tube and leave it to soak for a while. If it still doesn't budge, then it's down to the bike shop to let the heavy-handed mechanic have a look.

Fitting a new stem is simplicity itself: simply grease the quill very lightly to stop any corrosion, put a dab of grease on the threads of the expander bolt, and slide the stem into the steerer tube. How high or low you have your stem is up to you, but don't exceed the 'MAX HEIGHT' mark stamped on the side of the quill; if you want a higher position get a higher-rise stem instead of raising your current model to dangerous levels. At the other extreme, in trying to get a low position, some riders slide the stem right in to the weld on the underside of the forward extension. This can cause the stem to creak because the weld causes rocking in the headset locknut. If you want a low position, don't fit the stem so that the extension is any lower than ⅛in above the headset locknut.

Chris Young aboard his Pace RC-100, using his bar ends

The expander bolt should be tightened so that the stem is tight, but not so tight that the bars wouldn't turn in a crash.

Bar ends

Bar ends are one of those extras that have appeared on mountain bikes that make some of us wonder how we ever rode without them: they give a great climbing position, and a low-tuck cruising position on the flat. They come in two types: the cinch type fastening on the ends of the handlebar with an external clamp, in the same way as your stem clamps your bars, and the other type fastening in the ends of your bars with an expander wedge, as your stem clamps in your forks. With cinch types you must give up about 1in of your handlebars at each side; this can be gained either by sliding the grips and controls in further, or, if you have small hands, by trimming your grips down. Both types are easy to fit, but please remember to plug the exposed ends to reduce the risk of injuries occurring to yourself or to a friend in the event of a crash.

Setting it up right

Your bar and stem determine how your bike feels and handles. A longer stem puts more weight on the front wheel, changing the bike's handling characteristics. In extreme situations, too much weight on the front

Tim Gould's bike is set up to fit him like a tailored suit

wheel can result in it digging in and tucking under during cornering. If you're unsure if a stem is too long, use a plumb line to measure the horizontal distance from the centre of the grips to the centre of the front axle; measuring from the grips takes into account the handlebar bend. If the distance is less than 4in then the stem is too long, while more than 6in means that the bike will usually pop wheelies on climbs.

What all this means is that it isn't a great idea to set your bike up to fit you perfectly if it's going to compromise your bike's handling. There's no point in having a bike that fits you like your favourite shorts if it throws you off every time you go round a

corner or up a hill! Fortunately, provided that you're not a very funny shape and that you've been sold a bike that fits you, you should be able to get a comfortable position which still handles well. There's not one 'correct' position that you should be in when you're riding your bike, and some people like a longer, lower position than others. When pressed, experts usually say that your arms should be at around 90° to your body when you're sitting down. Consulting an experienced off-road rider is the best way to get advice for your particular bike and riding style. Bear in mind that the local terrain will influence your riding position – rocky, narrow tracks need a more upright style.

13: Saddles and seatposts

Choosing a saddle

The comfort of the saddle is the first thing most beginner mountain-bikers comment on. A comfy one makes riding a pleasure, but an uncomfy one is enough to put some riders off cycling for good. Though most riders spend quite a bit of time out of the saddle while riding, when you are sitting down the jarring from the trail far exceeds anything that a road rider has to endure. It makes sense for a mountain bike to have a more luxurious saddle than a road bike. Gels, foams and air bladders have all been developed to give you a smoother and more comfortable ride, and to stop you walking like John Wayne afterwards. Gel-padded saddles are great for the first-time rider, but tend to come with easily ripped lycra covers. If you can find a gel saddle with a tough leather or fake-leather cover, it'll last much longer than a lycra-covered saddle.

Different saddles suit different shaped bums, and what the young sales assistant in the shop says is dead comfy might give you more gyp than barbed-wire underwear. A look in the local shop will show you the bewildering array of different saddles available, and it's very difficult to assess what sort of saddle

An Avocet racing saddle (above) and a Specialized gel women's saddle

would suit you if it's sitting on a shelf in a box. Forward-thinking retailers could have one of each of their models for you to try, but normally they don't. So talk to similar-sized riders of the same sex about what saddles they use, and see if they'll lend you their saddles for a trial ride. Because women have wider pelvises on average, they need saddles with a broader rear section and a shorter length.

Good saddles come from Selle Italia and Avocet.

Seatposts

Because a mountain bike frame is smaller than a road bike's, it means that a longer seatpost is needed to attain the correct saddle position. A longer extension means greater stress for this component. Coupled with the extra shocks from the lumps and bumps off-road, this means that the cheap pressed-steel clamps that fit onto a plain alloy seatpost, common on very cheap bikes, don't work for any length of time off-road.

To allow correct saddle positioning, a micro-adjustable seatpost is standard on most bikes. This consists of a notched cradle which clamps onto a curved, grooved section on the seatpost. Tightening the Allen bolt passing through the clamp tightens the whole lot. To

remove the saddle from the seatpost, slacken the Allen bolt, usually with a 6mm Allen key, until you can turn the top cradle around, releasing the saddle. When replacing the saddle, this allows you to position the saddle rails on the lower half of the cradle, flip the top section back and clamp the whole lot together, all much quicker than piecing together the individual bits under the saddle.

The seatpost should be placed into the frame so that when it's set to your maximum height, it extends to 1in below the level of the top tube. I've seen Cannondale frames, in which the seat tube extends above the crossbar, snap because the seatpost hasn't gone far enough down the tube. The riders had relied on the 'MAX HEIGHT' mark on the seatpost, but because of the extended seat tube, the frames had snapped on the seat-tube extension. Tall riders beware!

Grease it

Your seatpost should slide smoothly in and out of your seat tube. If it doesn't, it means that the frame hasn't been finished properly at the factory: there'll be bits of steel sticking out, jamming the post in the frame. A well-equipped bike shop should have a seat-tube reamer, another workshop-only tool, to remove the jagged edges from the depths of

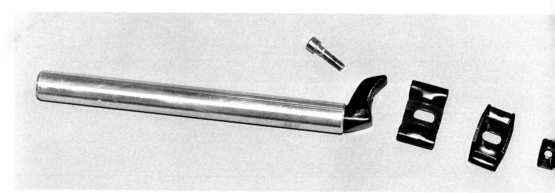

A dismantled seatpost

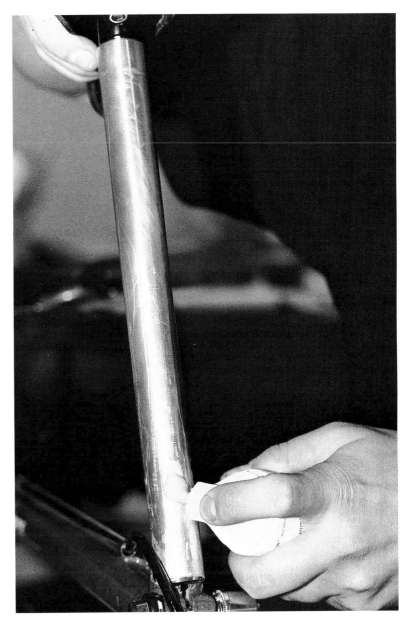

Tightening a seatpost. Seat position is just as important to comfort as seat design. Try various angles if your saddle's uncomfortable

Always grease the seatpost before insertion to avoid the post corroding in place

your frame. To ensure that your seatpost continues to slide properly, put a dab of grease around the bottom of the seatpost, so that it runs up the section of seatpost held in the frame. Wipe any excess away from the seat clamp.

Removing a seatpost

Seized seatposts can be the devil's own job to remove – yet another example of where a bit of maintenance can save you lots of time. If the post is corroded into the frame, penetrating oil sprayed down the gap between the frame and the post is the first thing to try. Keep putting oil in the gap, leave it overnight to soak and then try to loosen the post in the morning. If you still can't free the post by twisting the saddle, then you're going to have to sacrifice it for the sake of the frame. Most seatposts have a straight-sided clamp area, and additional twisting purchase can be got by using a big adjustable spanner or Stilson pipe wrench on the top of the post. If even that doesn't budge it, a pipe wrench at the bottom of the post may help things along.

If you still haven't got it out, you can try the following desperate measures. But beware – the bending and hammering involved can lead to a damaged frame, so if you're unsure, or not a good aim with a hammer, consult your local shop, the one with the mechanic who resembles prehistoric man.

The last resort but one is to try knocking the post a short distance downwards into the frame, to loosen it. Support the bottom bracket of the bike on blocks of wood. If the post can be knocked down in the frame, try again with the spanner or pipe wrench to twist it out. Finally, if all else fails, you can cut the seatpost off at the top of the frame and hammer the remainder down the seat tube far enough for you to get a new one in.

Saddle positioning

Just as important to comfort as choosing the correct saddle is the saddle position. Most male riders have the saddle set level, but if this doesn't suit your body shape or riding position, you may prefer to set it at a slight angle. Women generally find that positioning the saddle sloping forwards gives a more comfortable position.

Road riders have argued for years about the correct position and height for most efficient pedalling. Whereas a road bike is set up to extract the maximum amount of work from the rider's effort, a mountain bike has to take into account traction and weight distribution as well. The seat height should be set so that when the heel is put on the pedal at full extension, the leg is just locked out. Certainly, when in the normal pedalling position, with the ball of the foot on the pedal, there shouldn't be any rocking of the pelvis from side to side; this is only going to increase saddle-soreness.

Your seatpost has an adjustment for saddle position fore and aft, and it should be set up so that the small bump just below your kneecap on the outer side of your leg is either directly over the pedal spindle (forward position) or 2cm behind it (rearward position). Rearward saddle placement gives better traction and higher torque at lower-speed pedalling, whereas forward placement gives higher pedalling rates but less traction. Try your saddle in different positions and see which suits you best.

14: Frames

The frame of your bike is a remarkably lightweight structure considering the stresses it has to cope with. The tubes are plenty strong enough to allow you to plummet down hills or take big jumps in complete confidence that your frame won't fall apart, but they are susceptible to damage from being dropped against a wall or from big collisions. Though the tubes on most mountain bikes are large in diameter, most have walls about 0.7mm thick in the centre, with some going down as thin as 0.5mm. So you need to treat your bike with a degree of care to retain your frame's integrity and ensure it has a long and happy life.

This chapter covers the areas you should check every six months, and also after a big crash or a huge series of jumps, and before a mammoth cross-country trip, to make sure your bike won't fall apart on you when you're coming down the next big hill. Cleaning your frame won't make it work any better, but it does allow you to check that it will carry on working. Once much of the muck and grime is removed from the tubes, you can check the paintwork for any damage. There's no reason for a well-applied paint finish spontaneously to crackle up. What this usually means is that the tube or the joint under the paint has moved, cracked or crumpled. If so, you need to take it seriously.

Crash damage

Cars have a purpose-designed crumple zone so that in the event of a crash they absorb the impact of the collision. Bikes don't. When a bike is involved in a crash, its frame, fork and wheel can collapse under the strain. The areas most susceptible to crash damage are the joints where the top and down tube join the head tube. On aluminium bikes, the most usual point for a frame to break is on the underside weld on the joint between the head tube and the down tube. If there's a strange creaking from your headset on your aluminium bike, check this joint – aluminium has a habit of snapping suddenly rather than, like steel, bending first. As I said, paint doesn't usually just crack by itself, so any apparent paint crackling may indicate joint failure and should be referred to a competent dealer immediately. In some cases it may be possible to replace the tube, but if you're unlucky it's a new frame. Crash damage isn't usually covered by a manufacturer's warranty, so there's little point in complaining to the shop you bought your bike from that it didn't hold up well when you crashed into the sheer-sided ditch.

Dented tubes

Dents in your frame are usually caused either by dropping the bike against a wall, or by the

Check these areas for frame damage,
usually manifesting itself as crumpled or
cracked paint

handlebars spinning round in a crash and denting the top tube half-way along its length. There's not a great deal you can do about them. If the dent is big, take it along to your local framebuilder and see what he thinks. A dent much deeper than a few millimetres in a tube is probably big enough to start to affect frame strength, but it all depends on which tube, what tubeset, and where the dent is. Certainly a small dent isn't likely to cause any problems, and can be filled with automotive body filler and then touched up with paint.

Chainstay damage

Though the top of your right-hand chainstay may look a heck of a mess from the chain bouncing on it while you ride, it's rare for this to cause any structural frame damage. Most production frames usually have pretty thick-walled tubes for their chainstays, and though the outside of the tubes may look battle-scarred, they usually keep on working for a long, long time. Getting your framebuilder to fill the scars with brass doesn't make a lot of sense, as the heat needed to fill the grooves will affect the frame strength more than the scarring would.

The area of the chainstay most at risk from chain-induced damage is the area behind your chainrings where abrasions due to chainsuck can cause problems. Chainsuck is the habit your chainset can develop of keeping the chain on the rings when you change chainwheels, which results in the chain dragging itself between the rings and the chainstay. It's strange, but some people never get chainsuck and others are haunted by it. Thin steel chainrings and a clean drive train should alleviate the problem, but sometimes they don't. However, if you have

an elevated chainstay bike, or your frame has a chain deflector fitted next to the chainrings, you should be OK.

Repeated chainsuck can cause scarring of the chainstay, and on super-lightweight bikes this could cause the chainstay to snap from a stress fracture. Top UK framebuilder Dave Yates says that he's had to replace a couple of snapped chainstays on Tange Prestige frames, as Prestige has particularly thin tubing. Though this isn't the type of frame failure that would send you crashing to the ground, it could leave you stranded in the middle of nowhere with a frame not too receptive to pedalling.

Bent forks

After a front-end collision, the usual component to go is the front fork. Because of the strength of a wheel in impact, a fork can bend even if your front wheel remains perfectly intact. A fork can bend its blades, its steerer tube, or both. Which goes first depends on what sort of forks you've got. Bikes with oversize headsets usually bend the fork blades first, whereas bikes with 1in headsets and oversize blades will usually bend the steerer tubes first.

If the steerer tube on your forks is bent, it will cause the headset to be tight when pointed forwards but loose when positioned at 90° (see Chapter 10). If you're unsure whether your steerer tube is bent or not, remove the fork from the headset and check it by placing a straight-edge against the side of the steerer tube.

Checking fork-blade alignment is a little more tricky, though of course there are those occasions when you really don't need to get the straight-edge, as it's obvious the moment you pick yourself up off the floor. Many of

today's large-diameter, thin-walled forks will fail like a frame, with folded tube-wall and cracked paint being the tell-tale signs. A good quick check is to see if your brakes are still correctly set up to your front wheel. If the fork blades have moved then the brake will be off-line. Of course, this only works if the wheel has remained true and unbent. With forks you're just not sure about, try checking them from the side to see if they're in line with each other. If in doubt, go to a reputable dealer, or even a local framebuilder, to seek a second opinion. Whatever you do, *don't* continue riding on a bent fork, especially one you've bent straight again in order to get home, as the work-hardened steel will be much weaker and will have a tendency to snap at inopportune moments.

Frame alignment

If you've had a really big crash, there's a possibility that you could have bent your frame in a manner other than those described above. There could be no paint cracking, no tube folding, but your frame could be bent so that the front and rear wheels aren't in line, giving a bike which steers rather strangely. To check for this, run

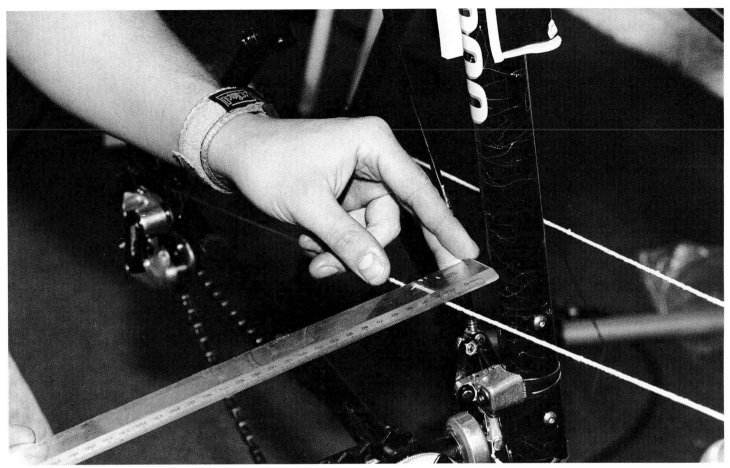

Measure the distance either side of the seat tube to the string. More than a few millimetres difference between each side means a bent frame

a length of taut string from the rear dropout, once round the head tube about half-way up, and back to the rear dropout. If your frame is perfectly on-track, the distance from these two lengths of string to the sides of your seat tube should be identical, though in practice most production bikes are usually 1 – 3mm off-track. Any more than this will adversely affect your bike's handling, and your frame will need re-setting by a competent builder, who will use a vice, a long length of tubing, a huge amount of brute force and a large amount of skill to get your frame back in a straight line. It might sound like a simple tweak, but it's knowing where to tweak the frame and how hard to pull. Don't try it at home!

Headtube damage

Occasionally, a badly machined headtube, or just one that's had downright hard riding, can stretch. The signs will be the headset cups rocking in the frame, and the bottom (usually) edge of the headtube being stretched out. This is another repair that can only be done by a well-equipped shop or framebuilder, as the usual method of repair is to machine down the headtube to cut out the stretched section, and then to reinstall

129

Beyond repair . . .

the headset. In extreme cases, a patch or reinforcing ring may have to be brazed onto the outside of the frame.

Scratch repair

Chromoly steel is reasonably rust-resistant but does need paint to protect it from the harsher aspects of the environment such as continuous damp or salted roads. It's rare for manufacturers to offer touch-up paint for their bikes, and it's rarer still for you to find a colour that matches your bike exactly. There's an easy way to keep your bike's paint in the same condition as the day you bought it: lock it in a darkened room! Scratches are a fact of life on a mountain bike, and most users are happy to let their bike accumulate minor nicks and scratches as it ages. However, for those really deep scratches caused by trailside scrapes, or by

vandals with a bunch of car-keys, touching up makes sense. Don't fill in the scratch with paint, but sand the affected area down to the metal with fine glasspaper, wipe the surface clean, then apply a thin layer of metal primer just on the area where the paint is removed, and leave it to dry for a day. Then apply the touch-up paint to the scratch in another very thin layer, and leave that to dry for another twenty-four hours. The whole painting and drying operation should take place in a warm, dry environment – rather than in your cold, damp garage – to ensure a smooth finish. Of course, touched-up scratches never blend in with the rest of the paint finish, which is why manufacturers sell stickers and offer their bikes with splatter paint finishes.

Repainting

After several years' use, your bike will look scruffy and tattered. You're then faced with either replacing the frame or repainting and refurbishing your current one. Both options have their advantages. A new frame will have up-to-date geometry, and maybe lighter and stronger tubing, but your old bike has memories and you know its handling traits. When you're getting your bike repainted, you could have a framebuilder braze on those little extras that you now realise you can't survive without. Extra water-bottle bosses, and relocated brake-bosses if you've an under-the-chainstay brake, can all be added before your bike is repainted.

As you'll have found, most manufacturers don't provide bikes with tough finishes. Riders wanting a long-lasting finish would be best advised to seek out an electrostatic powder coat finish, which will stay on your frame for ever and ever, only being removed by particularly nasty chemicals. A sprayed enamel finish is also tough, and beautiful to behold too, with possibilities ranging from a single-colour finish to considerable brush artistry – at a price. Whatever you do, don't take your bike to the local garage and ask the bloke who's more used to spraying Ford Cortinas to spray your lightweight frame; if it comes back without a huge dent somewhere on the frame, I'd be surprised. Bikes need special treatment when being painted, and they also need cleaning up afterwards. Threads need re-tapping, and the bottom bracket and headset will need facing again to accept their corresponding bearing cups. Dealing through a reputable shop or established framebuilder should avoid any problems that could occur.

Stop smiling, start walking!

15: Out on the trail

Many riders don't take any tools with them off-road, but trust to their bike's integrity and their own good luck. Others rely on their companions to bring along toolkits, as I did on a ride with several friends last summer. Crashing through bramble-infested tracks was a riot while it lasted, but eventually one of us got a puncture. Not to worry, we thought, as we helped Graeme replace his inner tube with the spare we'd brought. We'd just got Graeme's tube inflated with the CO_2 cartridges we were using, when another rider said 'Oh no, I've got a flat too!' Then, becoming wary, Graeme checked his front tyre and found he had another flat. Nearby was a field full of long, thick grass, so, recalling a tip we'd read in a magazine, we set about pulling bunches of grass from the field and stuffing tyres with them. No sooner had we got the two tyres stuffed than I got a flat too! Out with the grass again. The magazine said that grass-stuffed tyres gave a good enough ride to get back to civilization. Cushy the ride wasn't, and having tyres that snaked around on the rims didn't encourage high speeds on the several miles of switchback downhills we had to ride.

One spare tube and two CO_2 cartridges between four riders isn't sensible. Unless you're riding through a latex plantation there's no way of mending a flat tube in the wilds, and even fewer ways of inflating it. So take plenty of spares. And here are a few tips for repairing your bike when everything around you seems desperate.

Trail tool kit

The best trail tool kit you have is your home workshop. For rides in the rough stuff, if your bike is set up correctly, you shouldn't have any problems. Bikes don't spontaneously fall apart; bits come loose or work incorrectly because they haven't been set up right in the first place. For this reason it's important to maintain your bike thoroughly all the time. Riders who take the 'only fix it when it's broken' approach are tempting fate every time they journey out on a ride. Some riders complain that they don't want to be weighed down by a bunch of tools jangling around under their saddle; but it's easier to carry two pounds of tools than to carry your bike home when it breaks.

As I said in Chapter 2, there's no need to take your full tool kit out on the trail with you. The basic trail kit listed on page 19 will usually keep you rolling along when the mechanical gremlins hit. Because you can't take your full tool kit with you, it's important to keep your bike in good condition. Every week or so, check the tightness of your crank bolts and headset

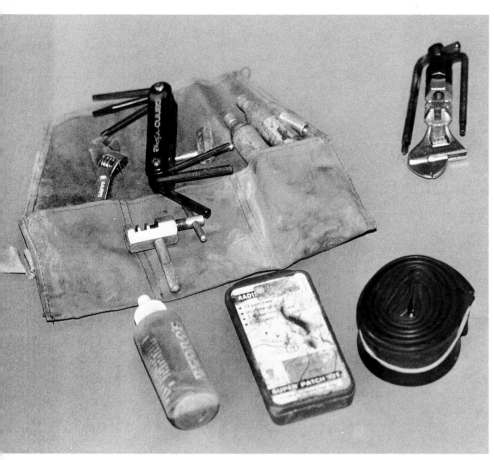

A trail tool kit

Extended trail tool kit

Of course, if you're going to climb the Himalayas, you'll need more than a few spanners and some zip ties. The extended trail tool kit should consist of these extra items:

- Headset and bottom-bracket spanners
- Crank puller
- 6in adjustable spanner
- Rear brake cable
- Rear gear cable
- Freewheel remover
- Two spare inner tubes
- Extra puncture repair kit
- Presta/Schrader valve adapter
- Schrader/Presta valve adapter
- Spare spokes

A pair of headset and bottom-bracket spanners weighs about 1lb, less than a full bottle of water, but provided that your fixed cup is tight and well fixed in your bottom bracket, any adjustment needed can be done on the adjustable cup with a nail and a large rock. Ideal it's not, but it'll save you a lot of weight, and fitting an Allen-key-adjustable headset and sealed cartridge bearing bottom bracket may be worth the money. The downside of cartridge bearing bottom brackets is that if the bearings pack up in deepest Tibet, you're going to be lucky to find a stockist of a 6003 neoprene-sealed bearing.

Depending on your disposition, there is one part that you either won't worry about at all or will cautiously carry round with you – the mechs. Thousands of miles from anywhere, a broken rear mech could mean a long ride in a ridiculous gear. That's fine if the terrain you have to cover is mostly flat, but you can't count on that. Packing a spare rear mech can save you a lot of getting off and pushing. A spare *front* mech would be considered a pessimistic luxury. It *might* get damaged, but

locknut. If your freewheel or freehub is making funny noises, then replace or adjust it. These are all jobs that require big, heavy tools, sometimes even including a vice, that really aren't practical to carry even on the most extended trips. To that end, manufacturers have released more user-friendly products such as headsets that can be adjusted with only an Allen key, and bottom brackets that use pressed-in sealed cartridge bearings which rarely fail catastrophically.

then your frame might break and you would need a frame torch to fix it, which could be tricky.

Broken spokes

Tourists carrying lots of gear over heavy terrain can suffer from spoke breakages, though these are pretty rare unless the wheel is very old. Before going on an extended trip it's worth visiting a good wheelbuilder to have your wheels checked. If a spoke breaks, it is usually one of those on the freewheel side of the rear wheel, and is impossible to remove without first removing the freewheel. There are some 'get-you-home' spokes on the market, designed to hook into the hole, from the centre of the hub, without the freewheel having to be removed first. You can make up for a broken spoke by adding more tension to the spokes around it, but if several spokes have been broken, then the only thing to do is to remove the freewheel and replace them.

Extra spares

It's practically guaranteed that every small village will have someone with a collection of large spanners and a vice. Barter, pay or beg them to help you mend your bike.

The alternative is to improvise. Someone with simple metalworking experience could make you up a piece of packing to allow you to use your headset spanner to remove your freewheel. If you desperately need to use a vice and can't find one, try packing out a drain cover with spanners and Allen keys, or any bits of metal you find lying around, to hold your freewheel remover in place. The more desperate your situation, the more ingenious you need to become.

US-based Pamir Engineering make super-small lightweight tools to remove Shimano freehub sprockets from their bodies. Their next-to-nothing light weight makes carrying them a lot of sense and since there's no other way of removing your freehub sprockets, a tool of this type is a worthwhile investment.

A crank puller, along with an adjustable spanner, will let you tighten or remove your crank arms, which is essential for bottom bracket work or if you've got a particularly jammed chain.

For extended trips in the back country, take a spare rear brake and rear gear cable. A rear gear cable can always be used on the front, but not vice versa, and the chance of finding a compatible gear or brake cable in the middle of nowhere is slim.

A more likely touring hazard is a three-inch gash in the sidewall of your tyre, which will render it useless, but thankfully one spin-off from the super-competitive world of mountain bike racing that benefits the tourist is the availability of folding tyres. Kevlar is used for the bead of racing tyres because it's much lighter than steel, but it allows the tyre to be folded up to about the size of a Coke can – they weigh in at less than 500g – and will get you out of a heap of problems.

The availability of mountain bike size tyres in many places is limited, in fact in some areas they are scarce and the further you're going, the greater the likelihood of punctures – if you don't have a tyre you can't ride any further and the same reasoning applies to the inner tubes. Along with the extra tubes, pack a few more patches than you normally would if you're really going to get away from it all. Taking valve adaptors will mean that if you do find a spare tube, but it won't work with your pump, you can screw on an adaptor and pump it up; by the same token if your pump becomes damaged, you can pump your tyres up with almost any pump you can find.

Frame failures

You can carry spares to put on your frame, but carrying a spare frame would be considered pessimistic in the extreme. I once cracked a rear dropout at the start of a two-week touring holiday, so I walked into the local Tourist Information centre and asked the assistant at the desk where I could find a welding kit! They were very helpful, and I found a garage who welded my dropout back together, allowing me to carry on riding. That was in 1987, and I've had several new bikes since then, but as far as I know that frame is still working fine today.

It's the question of reparability that is the big nail-in-the-coffin of many of the alternative materials on the market. Aluminium and bonded-steel framesets are coming into the mass market, where they usually offer a superb ride and low weight at a low price. However, for the expedition rider going miles from a cycle dealer, there's definitely an advantage in having a standard brazed-steel frame. In every town, be it in Nepal or Nigeria, someone will usually have a brazing torch and will be able to weld your bike back together if it cracks. That doesn't mean you can't tour on an aluminium bike, but if a problem develops, it's going to be hard to find a skilled TIG welder and heat-treating plant.

Broken rear mech

It's the most common problem, and also the most potentially disastrous for a mountain biker, when you've bent or broken your rear mech so that the chain won't run on the sprockets properly. Simply split the chain

and rejoin it so that it doesn't run through the rear mech any more, reducing your twenty-one-speed to a one-speed in a few minutes. Put the chain on the sprocket that gives the best straight alignment with the chainring you want to use at the front. This will give you either a super-low gear with a small chainring and a large sprocket, a medium-paced gear with middle/middle, or a downhill-all-the-way-home gear using the big ring.

Usually a bent rear mech means a bent gear hanger too. Check it, and if necessary fit a new one.

Of course, if you are going miles away from civilization, it's worth your while taking a spare rear mech. A cheap bottom-of-the-range model will cost you less, but will weigh more.

Crisped wheel

Sometimes you land so badly, or hit a ditch so deep, that you bend the wheel so hard it doesn't even turn in the frame. Chances are that you've damaged the rim beyond repair, so there's no point in pussyfooting about as you get the wheel sufficiently back into shape to let you ride it home. Take the wheel out of the frame, put it flat on the ground and hit it hard to force the rim roughly back where it should have been. Of course, if the wheel is only tweaked a bit, judicious use of your spoke key can get it spinning round again.

Bent forks

I've bent a few sets of forks in my time, and on every occasion have been able to ride home with them. If you pile your forks backwards, it may be that you can't ride because the front wheel is catching on the

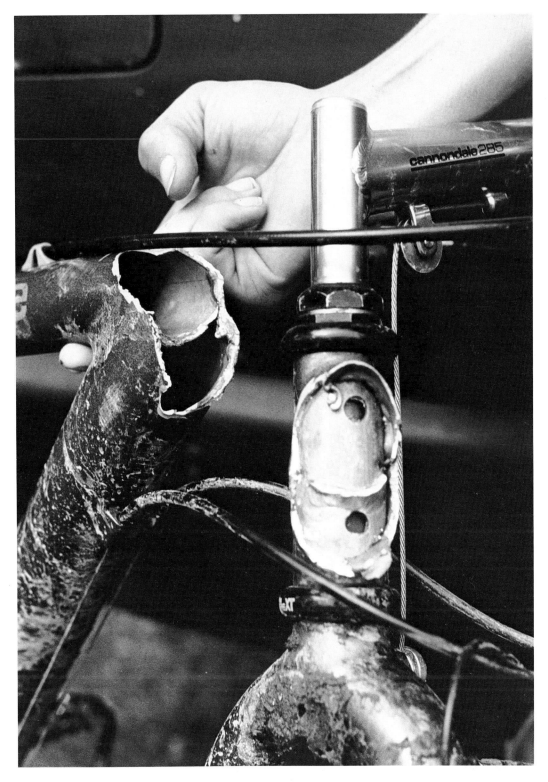

It's very uncommon for aluminium frames to break but when they do, they break in a big way!

A trashed rear wheel, meaning a long walk home

downtube, so you'll have to bend the blades forwards to give yourself enough room to turn the wheel. There's no 'correct' method for straightening bent forks, but it's best to pull on them hard rather than hitting them with something heavy. Replace them when you get home (see Chapter 14).

Ripped tyres

Sometimes you can rip the sidewall of a tyre when you puncture; then, when you reinflate the tyre, the inner tube will bulge out of the sidewall. If you ride like this for a while the inner tube will burst, but to prevent that happening you can put a patch on the inside of the tyre. Patches used to mend punctures can be used, but a piece of paper or card works just as well, sometimes better. Pop the piece of card in between the tyre and the tube, install the inner tube, pop the tyre back on the rim, and reinflate. As I mentioned on page 28, a spare lightweight folding tyre is compact to carry. It's a better solution than patching the tyre, and can save you a long walk home.

Chainrings

Sometimes you may hit a log or rock on the trail and bend a chainring, which may make pedalling impossible or throw the chain off when you try to use that ring. To straighten it, use an adjustable spanner to bend the ring

Straightening a chainring with an adjustable spanner

back at the point where it's fixed to the spider. This should make the ring straight enough to ride home, though it's unlikely you'll be able to get it straight enough to allow it to run without chain-rub on the front mech. The ring will be fatigued, and should be replaced promptly. It's unusual to bend anything other than the big ring when hitting a rock, though inner chainrings can sometimes get very badly mangled from chainsuck. If the worst comes to the worst, you usually have at least your middle ring to get home on. If your inner chainring is suffering from bad chainsuck, this is due to bent teeth or to scars on the side of the middle ring. If it's an alloy ring you can file the scars away with a rough rock, or even, as I did in one case, with the side of a matchbox.

Racks

If your bike's rack mounting bolts come loose and drop out, the Allen bolts that fit your bottle cages are probably the same thread, and can be used to replace them. If you haven't got enough bolts to go round, fit the ones you have in the dropout eye, and lash the top mounting point of the rack to the seatstays with heavy twine or a toe-strap. Racks sometimes break owing to the jarring they encounter off-road, but can be fixed with the help of a toestrap to lash the offending broken sections together; it's better to have a rack that works and no toestraps than not to be able to ride at all.

16: Ancillary equipment

As you'll have found when buying extra bits of kit for yourself, your bike is only a part of the investment you've made in mountain biking. The shorts, shirts, waterproofs and boots that a year-round rider needs can easily add up to several hundred pounds' worth, so it's just as important to keep this equipment in good condition.

Waterproofs

The most popular breathable waterproof fabric by far is Goretex, a micro-cellular membrane sandwiched between two layers of material. W. L. Gore, who produce Goretex, used the technology from their artificial heart-valve work to develop the fabric. Goretex works because the tiny perforations or pores in it let through water molecules in vapour form, but not the much bigger water droplets. Just like the pores of your skin, Goretex must be kept clean to ensure that it works properly, though the newer grades are much less susceptible to clogging than the first-generation material. To keep the pores clear, your sweaty, mudded-up jacket should be rinsed in lukewarm water after every couple of rides. You can wash Goretex clothing in a washing machine, but make sure you only use Goretex detergent and wash at a very low temperature, otherwise you may affect the proofing or sealing of the garment. Care must be taken when storing the material, too; the best idea is to hang it in a cool, dry cupboard. Folding it up and cramming it into the back of a drawer while it's still wet will quickly damage the fabric, causing the garment to leak. Of course, waterproofs made from other materials can also be cleaned, but none of them should be washed at high temperatures. And never use harsh detergents!

Other clothing

Sticking all your muddy clothing straight into the washing machine won't do your kit or your washing machine any good. In my garage I keep a large plastic dustbin which I fill with water after a particularly muddy ride to stick all my kit in overnight to get rid of the huge clumps of mud. Even after that, on the most intensive wash cycle, with the strongest biological washing powder, I can't shift the mud stains from my white socks.

If the ride you've been for isn't particularly muddy, do at least wash your shorts when you get back. Dirty shorts are a perfect breeding ground for the bacteria that cause saddle-sore infections. If possible, dry your shorts outside on the washing line, turned inside out so that the sun's ultraviolet rays can kill any remaining bacteria.

Footwear

Don't chuck your mucky boots in the garage when you get home from a ride; they'll be rotting away until you dig them out for next time. Rinse them under the tap to remove the large lumps of mud, then stuff them with newspaper and let them dry slowly, not in front of a roaring fire. Every couple of months, check the condition of the laces. While it's not catastrophic, it would be annoying to have a perfectly functioning bike and then a lace breaks on you in the middle of nowhere. Hey, there's another thing to add to your trail tool kit! One spare shoelace.

Helmets

Even if you haven't had a big crash, you should always check your helmet for any dings or dents: big ones mean you should replace it. You should take care of your helmet, and store it where it isn't going to get damaged by something dropping on it. If you can remove the pads from the inside of your helmet, give them a wash every couple of weeks to stop any nasty bugs growing in them.

If you've had a crash and hit your head, then the helmet will probably have been weakened. Replace it rather than risk riding around with inadequate protection; you never know when you'll need it.

Dirty but happy

Water bottles

Always rinse out your water bottles after use. Drinking from a dirty water bottle is a sure way to get a stomach upset. Bacteria love the damp close confines of the nozzle, and mould grows particularly well in the bottom of sticky water bottles. If you leave your bottle with a few drops of energy drink in the bottom, when you come back to it the next weekend there'll most likely be a big lump of mould grinning at you through the top. While mould isn't generally harmful, it doesn't taste too great, so to get rid of it use a long bottle brush. If necessary, use boiling water with a couple of teaspoons of bicarbonate of soda to loosen the mould first. Rinse the bottle thoroughly with clean water, drain it and leave it to dry.

A broken helmet, but an unbroken head

Trouble-shooting guide

Problem	Reason	Correction required
Chain no longer shifts smoothly from sprocket to sprocket.	1 Cables are dirty or stretched. 2 Chain is dirty or worn. 3 Rear mech or hanger is bent.	1 Clean and adjust the cables. 2 Clean and lubricate or replace the chain. 3 Straighten gear hanger and/or replace rear mech. See Chapter 5.
Chain doesn't shift smoothly from chainwheel to chainwheel.	1 Cables are dirty or stretched. 2 Chain is dirty or worn. 3 Chainwheels are loose or bent. 4 Front mech is bent or out of alignment.	1 Clean and adjust the cables. 2 Clean and lubricate or replace the chain. 3 Tighten chainwheel bolts, straighten or replace the chainrings. 4 Adjust front mech for alignment or replace. See Chapter 5 (Front mech) or Chapter 7 (Chainrings).
Chain slips when pedalling hard.	1 Chain worn. 2 Sprockets or chainwheel worn (especially with a new chain). 3 Rear mech out of adjustment. 4 Freewheel mechanism worn or broken.	1 Replace the chain. Chapter 5. 2 Replace sprockets and chainwheel. Chapters 7 & 8. 3 Adjust rear mech. Chapter 5. 4 Replace freewheel or freehub. Chapter 8.
Brakes don't work effectively.	1 Brake cables are dirty or stretched. 2 Brake blocks are worn. 3 Rims or blocks are greasy. 4 Brakes out of adjustment.	1 Clean and adjust the cables. 2 Replace the brake blocks. 3 Clean rims and blocks. 4 Adjust the brakes to their correct position. See Chapter 6.
Brakes squeak.	1 Brakes are not 'toed in'. 2 Rims or blocks are dirty. 3 Brakes are loose on their pivots. 4 Some brakes always squeak!	1 Adjust the brakes so that the front edge of the pad hits the rim first. 2 Clean the rims and blocks. 3 Tighten the pivot bolts. 4 Buy new brakes, pads or earplugs! See Chapter 6.

Problem	Reason	Correction required
The bike doesn't steer 'properly'. It feels like it's wobbling.	1 Headset is loose. 2 Wheel cones are loose. 3 Stem out of line. 4 Frame cracked or bent.	1 Adjust the headset. Chapter 10. 2 Adjust wheel cones. Chapter 8. 3 Straighten the stem. Chapter 12. 4 Examine the key frame breakage areas and consult a reputable dealer. Chapter 14.
Pedalling is irregular.	1 Crank arm is loose. 2 Pedal bearings are loose. 3 Bottom bracket bearings are loose. 4 Crank, bottom bracket or pedal is bent.	1 Tighten the crank bolt. Chapter 7. 2 Adjust the pedal bearings. Chapter 11. 3 Adjust the bottom bracket bearings. Chapter 7. 4 Replace the bent part. Chapter 7 or 11.

Recommended parts and equipment

Across the price range, there are many different choices of equipment if you want to replace an item or upgrade your bike. In mountain biking, just like most other things, it's usually a case of 'you get what you pay for'. More money buys lighter, stronger, better-functioning equipment. Though many of the parts of a mountain bike are a very personal choice, and reflect your riding style and the type of terrain you usually cover, here are a few points to consider when replacing or upgrading equipment.

Gears

Shimano's Hyperglide is fabulous. Its problem lies in the fact you have to buy the complete Shimano system of hub, cassette, gear mechanism, chain and thumbshifters, and this inflexibility has led some people to go for SunTour drive chain components, which allow you to use any hub in conjunction with a screw-on freewheel. SunTour's new Micro-Drive system, however, requires a SunTour cassette. Hyperglide out-shifts everything on the market at the moment, and the more expensive groupsets such as DX and XT shift better for longer.

Cantilevers

Shimano's standard brakes are OK, but the most popular replacement brake on the market is the DiaCompe 986. It's a super-small cantilever that works well and weighs very little. They're a much more reasonable price than the super cantilevers, such as Graftons, IRD Switchbacks and Marinnovative Decelerators. These work very well, but require a high degree of accuracy in setting up and maintenance, and they cost a lot!

Brake levers

The DiaCompe SS-5 levers are some of the best on the market. They're basically a refined BMX brake lever and are excellent value for money. There's nothing intrinsically wrong with the standard brake levers from standard groupsets, but with the honourable exception of XTR they're usually nothing to write home about either.

Saddles

The Selle Italia Turbo is a classic standard saddle, but you need tough buttocks as it's not the best-padded saddle in the world. Top of the heap in the saddle department is the Selle Italia Titanium Flite, a minimalist racing saddle offering a surprising degree of comfort.

Pedals

Shimano's SPD pedal system is a favourite with hard-core riders and racers. It takes some time to get used to, but the benefits of not having to fiddle with toestraps are well worth the effort. The Deore DX SPD pedals work very well and are actually stronger than XTs, though they do weigh a little more. SunTour make some of the nicest standard pedals, and the SR Low Fat is an excellent mid-priced pedal. Specialized make the best toeclips.

Grips

The ODI Attack grip designed by John Tomac is a favourite with riders of all levels: the thin rubber ribs give a comfortable grip and disperse sweat quickly. Onza's Porcipaws grip is popular with hard-core riders and those wanting a small diameter grip.

Tyres

For hard dirt, Specialized's Ground Control Extremes are superb. In wet conditions, Onza Porcupines work very well, and the Panaracer Smoke is a superb tyre in anything other than super-dry conditions. The new 1.9in Smoke could be the best tyre ever when it finally goes on general release.

Light tyres mean faster acceleration. Kevlar-beaded tyres are the lightest around, and you can actually feel the difference in responsiveness.

Further reading

It is impossible to cover all aspects of mountain bike maintenance in this book. On the market there are several well established, excellently written volumes to help keen mechanics take their maintenance skills a stage further.

Barnett's Manual
Probably the most useful is *Barnett's Manual – Analysis and Procedures for Bicycle Mechanics*. It's incredibly detailed, and is like having a pro-team mechanic at your side twenty-four hours a day.

Sutherland's Handbook for Bicycle Mechanics
A suitable volume to accompany *Barnett's* is *Sutherland's Handbook for Bicycle Mechanics*. It's currently in its fifth edition, and has comprehensive details of all aspects of bicycle components. It gives hints on how to mend parts, but it's most useful when information is needed about a product. Its wheelbuilding section covers most hubs and rims available, allowing you to calculate spoke length for any combination and any spoking pattern.

The Bicycle Wheel
Jobst Brandt's *The Bicycle Wheel* is the most complete book on wheelbuilding. It covers the historical and technical aspects of wheels, and is the bible for many pro builders. *Sutherland's Handbook* is an essential accompaniment to it, because of its details of wheel combinations.

Richards' Mountain Bike Book
Written by one of the original pioneers of mountain biking, Charlie Kelly, with a supplementary expedition section by Nick Crane, this book deals with the development of the sport in detail and with a hint of irreverence. Highly recommended coffee-table reading.

Mountain Bike Magic
How to get the Most out of Your Mountain Bike
By Rob van der Plas, this book emphasizes the charms of mountain biking. The excellent colour illustrations show in detail how to handle your bike under all conceivable circumstances. Technical information is restricted to that necessary for selecting components and keeping the bike in tune.

The Mountain Bike Book
Choosing, Riding and Maintaining the Off-Road Bicycle
Another of Rob's books, this is a concise manual on the mountain bike and its use. The emphasis is on the technical aspects with clearly illustrated instructions.

Index